Becoming the Seed

BECOMING THE SEED

—

Lessons from a Tamil Farmer

on Building, Belonging, and Coming Home

ARUN RAJIAH

TITLE: Becoming the Seed SUBTITLE: A Journey of Growth, Failure, and the Quiet Wisdom of a Farmer's Grandson

Copyright

Copyright © 2024, 2026 by Arun Rajiah

All rights reserved. No part of this publication may be reproduced, distributed, or transmitted in any form or by any means, including photocopying, recording, or other electronic or mechanical methods, without the prior written permission of the publisher, except in the case of brief quotations embodied in critical reviews and certain other non-commercial uses permitted by copyright law.

Third Edition

ISBN: 979-8-304-40176-0

Published in Chennai, India, and distributed internationally.

The stories in this book are true. Some names and identifying details have been changed to protect the privacy of founders and families who trusted me with their journeys. Where a founder has given permission to use their real name, I have. Where I have changed the name, I have also slightly changed the context so the person remains unrecognizable even to those who know them.

Dedication

For my Thatha Seeni, who taught me how to grow, and how to wait.

Contents

Introduction: A Different Kind of Growth

PART ONE: THE EARLY SEEDS
Chapter 1: The Soil of Beginning
Chapter 2: Breaking New Ground
Chapter 3: The Nature of Growth

PART TWO: CULTIVATING WISDOM
Chapter 4: The Ethics of Growth
Chapter 5: Planting Alongside — On Co-founders and the Companion Crop
Chapter 6: The Hidden Seeds
Chapter 7: The Weight of the Seeds

PART THREE: HARVESTING PURPOSE
Chapter 8: Reading the Weather — On Money, Investors, and the Storm Seasons
Chapter 9: Growing Through Seasons
Chapter 10: Return to Simplicity
Chapter 11: The Farmer's Solitude — On Inner Life, Family, and Identity
Chapter 12: Growing Others

Seeds for Tomorrow

A Note on Terms for the International Reader

Acknowledgments

About the Author

Acknowledgments

This book, like any good harvest, is the result of many hands and hearts working together. Just as my grandfather taught me that no farmer works alone, this book grew from the support, wisdom, and patience of many people, on several continents.

First, my deepest gratitude to my family. To my wife, who believed in this farmer's grandson when the world gave her every reason not to, who sat through those long conversations about leaving a secure job for the unknown, who held things together during the lean seasons when the harvest had not yet come, and who has read every draft of this book, including the bad ones. To my children, who have grown up watching their father talk to founders late into the night and have asked the sharpest questions of anyone.

To the founders across India, Singapore, Dubai, London, Berlin, Lagos, Nairobi, Cape Town, Tokyo, New York, and Atlanta who shared their journeys with me, allowing their stories to become part of this narrative. Some of you called at midnight. Some of you sat across from me in coffee shops with trembling hands and wild ideas. Some of you failed spectacularly and came back stronger. Some of you failed and did not come back, and I think of you, too. This book exists because you trusted me with the parts of your lives you could not show your investors, your teams, or sometimes your families.

To the readers of the earlier editions who wrote to me from places I had never been, reminding me that the farm in Theni speaks a language understood in rice paddies and wheat fields, vineyards and olive groves everywhere. Your letters pushed this third edition into being.

To the small circle of entrepreneurs and mentors who still teach me daily, in formal settings and informal ones, you show me that wisdom, like good soil, grows richer when it is shared and poorer when it is hoarded.

Most importantly, to Thatha, who never read these pages but whose wisdom fills every one of them. Your lessons continue to grow and bear fruit in ways you could not have imagined, in countries whose names you could not pronounce, in the hands of founders you would have liked very much.

Arun Rajiah Chennai, 2026

Introduction: A Different Kind of Growth

Most people think entrepreneurship begins with a brilliant idea, or a detailed business plan, or a founder who sees what others miss. That is not wrong, exactly, but it is not the beginning. In my experience, entrepreneurship begins earlier, and quieter, and much further from any conference room.

For me, it began in a district called Theni.

Theni is a small place in the southern Indian state of Tamil Nadu, tucked against the Western Ghats mountain range where the air smells of cardamom and the earth holds generations of farming memory. If you are reading this book in Iowa or Gauteng, in Munich or São Paulo, you may never have heard of Theni, and there is no reason you should have. But you have a Theni of your own. It might be a wheat farm in Kansas, or a goat pasture in the Peloponnese, or a great-aunt's kitchen in Seoul where the rhythm of daily work taught you something you have not yet named. Whatever that place is for you, it will understand what this book is trying to say.

I am an entrepreneur and a mentor. I have built companies that failed, companies that survived, and companies that became things I did not intend. I advise founders now, across India and beyond — people I meet at conferences in Singapore, on video calls with Berlin, in quiet evening walks with founders visiting Chennai on business. After two decades of this work, the best guide

Becoming the Seed

I ever had was not a book, not a professor, not a Silicon Valley blog. It was my grandfather, my Thatha Seeni.

Thatha is the Tamil word for grandfather. Seeni was his name. He was an unlettered farmer who never sat in a classroom and never learned to read, and who nevertheless had more useful wisdom about building things than any MBA I have ever met. He would say things, standing in his fields with soil between his fingers, that I would spend years trying to unpack.

"A farmer cannot force the rain to fall or the sun to shine. All he can do is prepare the soil, plant the seeds, and nurture them with care and patience."

Entrepreneurship, I now believe, mirrors this reality. Founders cannot control markets or customers or global disruptions, any more than a farmer can control the weather. What we can do is prepare, plant, tend, and wait. And when conditions turn against us, as they always eventually do, what remains is whatever we have built into the soil itself.

This is not a how-to guide. If you are looking for a chapter on Series A fundraising tactics or a framework for product-market fit, there are excellent books for that, written by people more qualified than I am. This book is something different. It is a collection of stories from an entrepreneur's life, braided together with a farmer's lessons, organized loosely around the arc of becoming. It is about the early seeds of who we are, the hidden seeds that bring later trouble, and the seeds we eventually plant in others.

Becoming the Seed

I have tried, in this third edition, to write the book as honestly as I can. I have included failures I used to skip over. I have included moments when my advice to founders was wrong, and when my own ventures collapsed for reasons I only understood in retrospect. I have tried to let my grandfather be a real person and not a saint, because he was a real person and not a saint, and sanctifying him would dishonor him.

Most of the founders in this book are real. Some are identified by their real names. Many are composites or have had their details changed to protect privacy, because founders who spoke to me did so in vulnerable moments and deserve that protection. When you read that a founder's metrics tripled or that a pivot worked beautifully, know that the story is true but the numbers are sometimes rounded and the timeline compressed, the way all stories work when told well.

A word to the international reader. The book is set primarily in India, because that is where I have lived and built and failed. But the soil I am describing is not exclusively Indian soil. I have tried to gloss the Tamil and Hindi terms on first use, and I have included, in the later chapters, founders I have worked with in Dubai, Dublin, Lagos, Berlin, Tokyo, Cape Town, Atlanta, and Singapore. Their stories are here because they belong here: the principles Thatha taught me did not stop at the border of Tamil Nadu, and it would be a poor testament to his wisdom if I pretended otherwise.

What you will find in these pages is real stories of attempts and failures, of learning and growth, of finding purpose in unexpected places. You will see how the practical wisdom of a man who never went to school provided better guidance for my entrepreneurial journey than many modern business theories. You will see some mentoring stories that went well, and some that did not. You will see me at my best and at my worst, and both are important.

This is a story about understanding that success is not always what we think it is, that failure is often our greatest teacher, and that sometimes the most profound wisdom comes from the simplest observations. Like a farmer watching over his fields, trusting that with care and patience, growth will come.

Thatha often said, "The sun and the soil do not need complicated explanations. They just need attention and respect."

In moments of doubt, I still return to his words: "You cannot pull a plant from the soil to make it grow faster. All you can do is ensure it has everything it needs."

In the end, both the farmer and the entrepreneur understand one profound truth: the harvest is only as good as the care given to the seed. And the seed is only as good as the care given to the farmer who tends it.

That is what this book is about. Becoming the seed, and becoming the farmer who tends it, and, eventually, becoming someone who tends others.

Becoming the Seed

PART ONE: THE EARLY SEEDS

Chapter 1: The Soil of Beginning

Life has a peculiar way of teaching its lessons. In the small town of Theni, where the Western Ghats paint the horizon and cardamom-scented breezes drift through narrow streets, I was known as the boy who could not study. The "worst student," they called me. Teachers would shake their heads, their expressions a mixture of disappointment and resignation.

I remember the exact shape of those looks. Mrs. Lakshmi, my mathematics teacher, had a particular way of pressing her lips together when she returned my test papers, as if holding back words that would hurt too much to say aloud. "Arun," she would say, "you have to try harder." But I was trying. The numbers simply refused to arrange themselves in any order that made sense to me. They sat on the page like seeds scattered by wind.

Every morning, while other students rushed to the tuition centers that dot small-town India, I would find myself drawn instead to our family farm. There, amidst the gentle rustle of curry leaves and the earthy scent of freshly tilled soil, my real education began. My grandfather, my Thatha Seeni, saw something in me that report cards and test scores could not measure.

He had never gone to school himself, but he had a way of understanding life that no textbook could teach. While working in his fields, he would point to things others might miss. How ants worked together to carry food. How certain plants grew stronger after being cut back. How the morning sun made some crops flourish while others needed afternoon shade.

"See this?" he said one morning, holding up a handful of rich, dark soil near the irrigation channel. Then he walked twenty paces east and scooped up another handful, lighter, sandier. "Same field. Different soil. A foolish farmer plants the same thing everywhere. A wise farmer reads each handful."

I did not understand then. Years later, sitting in boardrooms and coffee shops with founders from every background, I would think about those two handfuls of soil. Every market has its own texture. Every team has its own texture. Every customer has its own texture. The founders who fail are often the ones planting the same seed everywhere and expecting identical results.

The Thinnai

The *thinnai* of our home became my first classroom. A thinnai is a raised stone platform attached to the front of a traditional South Indian house, usually shaded by a tiled overhang or a neem tree. It serves the function that a porch serves in the American South, or a veranda in colonial architecture, or a stoop in Brooklyn. It is where family and neighbors gather in the evenings to talk, to drink coffee, to watch the day end.

Ours was a cool slab of granite, worn smooth by three generations of sitters. Here, as the evening sun painted the sky in shades of orange and purple, Thatha would share observations that seemed simple at first but contained profound truths about life, work, and growth.

The thinnai was more than a porch. It was the village's living room. Neighbors would stop by after the day's work, settling onto the cool stone with a groan of tired muscles. The women would bring filter coffee in small steel tumblers. Children chased each other around the courtyard. And in the middle of it all, Thatha would sit cross-legged, his white *dhoti* — the long cotton wrap worn by most older men in Tamil Nadu — folded neatly at his knees, dispensing wisdom the way the neem tree in our yard dispensed shade, generously, without being asked.

Patience and Observation

Patience was the first virtue I learned. Farming is not an instant-gratification business. Seeds are sown with hope, but growth happens silently under the soil. I remember watching my grandfather planting seeds and hearing him say, "Don't disturb the soil every day to see if it is growing. Some things grow only when left alone."

Observation followed patience. You had to notice the slightest change in the color of leaves, the dampness of the soil, the behavior of pests.

One afternoon, as the sun hung heavy in the sky, I remember Thatha kneeling beside a struggling tomato plant. Its leaves had wilted, and the soil around it looked parched. "Do you see?" he asked, pointing at the cracks in the soil. "This plant isn't weak. It's just thirsty." With gentle hands, he created small channels in the soil, letting water trickle down to the roots. Within days, the plant had perked up, its leaves reaching for the sun again.

I think about that tomato plant often. I have seen startups that looked dead, with their teams demoralized, their products stalling, their investors losing interest. Sometimes the problem was not that the company was weak. It was thirsty for something specific. A different go-to-market approach. A single key hire. A conversation with the right customer. The founders who survived were not the ones who ripped everything out and started over. They were the ones who, like Thatha, knelt down close enough to see the cracks and made small channels for water to reach the roots.

Another lesson in patience came during harvest season. I recall a day when I eagerly pulled a carrot from the soil before it was fully mature. The result was a small, underdeveloped vegetable, half-formed, pale. Thatha chuckled, patted my shoulder, and said, "Everything has its time. The soil gives when it's ready."

That image stayed with me as I later navigated the world of startups, understanding that success cannot be forced before its time. I have watched founders raise money too early, launch products too soon, expand into markets they were not ready for. All variations of pulling the carrot. There is a particular kind of heartbreak in watching a good idea die because it was rushed. The product had potential, the team had talent, but someone, usually a well-meaning advisor or an impatient investor, said, "You need to scale now." And the carrot came out of the ground half-formed.

The Year Thatha Was Wrong

I want to pause here, because if I keep telling Thatha stories where he is always right, this book will become a fairy tale. He was not always right.

One year, Thatha became convinced that we should plant a particular variety of millet across most of our land. He had heard about it from a traveling merchant who had seen it grown successfully in the north. Thatha was so taken with the idea that he cleared two fields for it and planted them during what he judged to be the right window.

The crop failed. Not dramatically, not tragically, but in the slow, disappointing way that some crops fail: the yield was small, the grains underdeveloped, the quality poor. We lost the season's labor on those two fields.

What I remember most is not the failure. It is the week after, when Thatha walked the failed fields every morning and afternoon for seven days, hands behind his back, saying nothing. On the eighth day, he sat down on the thinnai in the evening and said, only to me, "I wanted to believe the merchant. I didn't read the soil before planting. I wanted the harvest more than I respected the field."

That confession has stayed with me longer than any of his wise sayings. Because wisdom without failure is performance, not wisdom. The reason Thatha's advice was worth anything was that he had been wrong, he knew he had been wrong, and he carried that knowledge into every subsequent decision.

I have thought about this in my own life many times. When a mentee asks me for advice and I speak too confidently, I sometimes hear Thatha on the thinnai that evening: *I wanted the harvest more than I respected the field.* And I slow down.

Adapting to Uncertainty

Farming taught me about uncertainty. One season would bring a bountiful harvest. The next might be ruined by unseasonal rains. Thatha did not panic when this happened. He adapted. If one crop failed, he planted another more suited to the conditions.

In my entrepreneurial journey, I have faced similar situations. A product launch would fail. A client would back out. Funding would dry up. Just like the farm, I learned to adapt, pivot, and try again with a renewed focus.

I recall a time when heavy rains flooded our fields. The crops were destroyed, and the loss weighed heavily on the family. But instead of mourning the loss for long, Thatha began planting water-resistant varieties in the patches that could still hold moisture. It was not a perfect solution, but it ensured we had some yield to fall back on.

What struck me was not the planting itself. It was the speed. Thatha did not call a meeting. He did not make a spreadsheet. He walked the flooded fields at dawn the very next morning, feeling the soil with his bare feet, sorting waterlogged sections from salvageable ones in his head. By noon, he had a plan. By evening, he was planting.

Years later, when a global pandemic shut down the economy overnight, I thought about Thatha walking those flooded fields. The founders who survived were not the ones with the best contingency plans on paper. They were the ones who, like Thatha, walked their own ruined fields the very next morning and started replanting before the water had fully receded. One founder I was mentoring in Bengaluru had her entire events business evaporate in the first week of the pandemic. Within a month she had pivoted to virtual event production, hired three of the freelancers whose income had also vanished, and was breaking even again. She did not have better strategy than her competitors. She had faster feet.

The Reservoir

Thatha often spoke about resilience. "Nature always gives us another chance," he would say. During one particularly dry season, he focused on building small reservoirs to trap rainwater. It was backbreaking work, digging by hand in sun-hardened soil, shaping the banks with nothing more than a shovel and stubborn faith. The other farmers watched and shook their heads. "Why waste energy on holes in the ground when there's no rain to fill them?" they said.

Years later, those reservoirs saved our crops during an unexpected dry spell. The same farmers who had mocked him came to ask whether they could share the water. Thatha did not gloat. He simply opened the channels and let the water flow into their fields too.

"Water does not know whose field it is feeding," he said.

That lesson — invest in infrastructure before you need it, and share the returns when you have them — has proven true in every business I have built or advised. The founders who build systems when the company is small look paranoid in year one. They look like geniuses in year three. The founders who build relationships with their community when they have little to offer are the ones whose communities show up when the crisis comes.

The Cracked Tool

One evening, under a sky painted with crimson and gold, I sat beside Thatha as he worked on repairing an old wooden tool. "This tool has served me for years," he said. "But it needs care to keep going."

He turned the handle in his hands, running his thumb along a crack in the wood. "See this? If I had oiled it last season, this crack wouldn't be here. Small things become big things when you ignore them."

He was talking about a plough handle, but he could have been talking about co-founder relationships, or the slow drift between a CEO and her earliest employees, or the small resentments that build between business partners who stop communicating. In the companies I advise now, the biggest catastrophes almost never come from sudden shocks. They come from small cracks left untended for too long. A difficult conversation postponed for a month becomes a conversation postponed for a quarter. The trust frays. The crack widens. One morning someone quits.

Lessons from the Farm, for Anyone

Reading these stories back, I am aware that you may not have grown up on a farm. Most readers will not have. But the principles are not about farming. They are about the patience of growing things, the humility of reading conditions you cannot control, and the discipline of preparing for futures you cannot predict.

A Kenyan coffee farmer would recognize what Thatha was doing with the reservoir. A vintner in Bordeaux would recognize the reading of soil. A baker in Oaxaca who sources her masa from small growers would understand the network of mutual obligation that the tomato harvest created in our village. These are not Tamil lessons. They are lessons any culture that has grown things slowly and traded with its neighbors will recognize.

The deeper wisdom of entrepreneurship is not industry-specific and not even economy-specific. It is agricultural, in the oldest sense of the word. You are tending something living. You are subject to weather. You are one actor in a larger ecosystem. And you will be judged, in the end, not by the size of one harvest but by the condition of the soil you leave behind.

Reflections on Growth

Looking back, I realize that every stage of life resembled a farming cycle: preparation, planting, growth, harvest, and rest. The soil of my beginnings was rich with love and wisdom, and it continues to nourish me today.

Growth is not always linear. Sometimes you grow sideways, taking unexpected paths. But as long as you are anchored in the right soil, you will bear fruit.

In those quiet fields of Theni, with the scent of earth and the wisdom of an old farmer, my journey began. It is a journey I continue to walk, one seed, one lesson, one season at a time.

Seeds to Plant

Before each chapter ends, I will offer a few questions. They are not homework. They are seeds. You can leave them in the ground for as long as you want, or you can dig them up and plant them today. That is your choice.

For this chapter, three questions to sit with:

What was the farm of your childhood? What was the place, or the person, that taught you how to grow before anyone taught you anything else?

What is one "carrot" you have pulled too early in your career? What did it cost you, and what did it teach you?

Becoming the Seed

If you had to describe the soil you are building on right now — your team, your market, your relationships — in one honest sentence, what would that sentence be?

Chapter 2: Breaking New Ground

The journey from Theni to Chennai felt like stepping from a small stream into an ocean. Armed with nothing but a diploma, determination, and Thatha's wisdom, I found myself navigating the bustling lanes of Richie Street, the computer hardware district of Chennai, Tamil Nadu's capital city on the Bay of Bengal. In 2003, computers were still considered luxury items in most Indian households, each purchase a major family decision. Chennai's relentless pace and the metallic hum of progress were a stark contrast to the sunlit fields of Theni, yet Thatha's lessons stayed with me.

I arrived at Chennai Central Station on a Tuesday morning with a vinyl bag, two thousand rupees in my pocket, and the phone number of a distant cousin who worked in a printing shop near Parry's Corner. The train had taken twelve hours. I had not slept. The station swallowed me whole: the noise, the crush of bodies, the auto-rickshaw drivers shouting destinations I had never heard of. For the first time in my life, I understood what it felt like to be a seed torn from its soil.

If you have ever moved from a smaller town to a big city — from Lagos to Abuja, from Chiang Mai to Bangkok, from a Ukrainian village to Kyiv, from an Ohio mill town to Manhattan — you will know the particular loneliness of that first week. The streets do not know you. The streets do not care that they do not know you. You are one more body in a current.

Becoming the Seed

My cousin's one-room apartment in Tondiarpet, a working-class neighborhood in northern Chennai, became my home for those first weeks. Four of us shared that room: my cousin, his colleague, a student from Kerala, and me. We slept on mats rolled out each night and rolled up each morning to make space for living. The communal bathroom down the hall served eight families. The walls were thin enough to hear every conversation, every prayer, every argument.

I had not come to Chennai for comfort. I had come to grow.

The First Job

My first job was at a small computer hardware shop. I earned eight hundred rupees per month, which in 2003 was enough to keep my dreams alive if I was careful. The shop owner, Rajan *anna* — *anna* is the Tamil word for "older brother," used as a term of respect for a man somewhat older than oneself — was a gruff man with a tobacco-stained smile who ran his business from a narrow stall sandwiched between a mobile phone repair shop and a seller of pirated CDs. The stall was barely ten feet wide, stacked floor to ceiling with motherboards, RAM sticks, and power supply units in their original cardboard boxes.

During my first week, I encountered a customer who changed my perspective on sales forever. He was not just looking for a computer. He was looking for a solution to a problem. While my colleagues eagerly displayed the latest models with advanced specifications, I paused and asked him a simple question:

"What do you need it for?"

The customer was a thin, anxious man in his fifties named Suresh. He ran a small grocery store in North Chennai and needed something reliable for accounting. More importantly, he needed a system simple enough for his elderly father to operate. We settled on a basic, affordable system, one that cost him far less than his original budget.

I spent an extra hour that evening setting up the computer at his shop, three streets away. I installed the accounting software, typed up a one-page guide in Tamil, and showed his father how to open the program and enter numbers. The old man's face lit up when the screen responded to his keystrokes. "It works!" he said, as if a miracle had occurred.

Two weeks later, Suresh returned with three other shopkeepers from his neighborhood. They were not looking for the most expensive computers. They wanted reliable tools to ease their workload.

That evening, during a call home, I shared the story with Thatha. After a long pause, he said, "Remember how we planted cheaper vegetable varieties near the village path? Not because they were less valuable, but because they were what our neighbors needed most."

Rajan anna noticed the steady stream of shopkeeper customers coming in and asking for me by name. He did not say anything for weeks. One evening he pulled me aside and handed me an extra two hundred rupees. "Don't let it go to your head," he said. But I saw his expression. It was the same look Thatha got when a plant he had been tending finally bore fruit.

The Time I Overcharged a Customer

Before I keep romanticizing my Richie Street days, I have to tell you about the time I cheated a customer. It was an accident in intent but not in effect, and I carry it still.

A young man came in, maybe my age at the time, looking for a used laptop. He did not know what he was looking at. I could tell from the first thirty seconds. He had received a small loan from his uncle and wanted to impress his new employer by showing up with a laptop of his own. The particular model he had asked about was sitting in our inventory at a price we could not move. Rajan anna had been trying to clear it for two months.

I sold it to him. At the full asking price, which was above market. I remember telling myself, during the sale, that I was doing Rajan anna a favor by clearing inventory. I remember telling myself that the young man was getting a real machine, which was true. I remember telling myself that he would have overpaid somewhere else too, which was also probably true. All of those justifications were true in the moment, and all of them were beside the point.

The point was that I had information he did not have, and I used it against him instead of for him.

Two weeks later he came back. Not angry. Confused. The laptop had a known defect with its display that I had not disclosed, not because I knew for certain but because I had not bothered to check. He asked if I could help. I replaced the screen at cost, worked on it for three evenings, and gave it back to him without charging my labor. He shook my hand and thanked me warmly. He had no idea how badly I had handled the sale.

I did not tell Thatha about this for years. When I finally did, during one of my visits home, he listened without expression. Then he said, "The young man didn't learn anything from that exchange. You learned the whole lesson. That's the interest you will pay on the loan."

I still think about that sale when someone tells me that business is amoral, or that founders do not have to choose between ethics and survival. I have chosen poorly before. The cost was not the money. The cost was that I had to spend the next twenty years proving to myself that I was not the kind of person who made that choice. That is a long interest payment on a small loan.

Juggling Many Roles

Life in Chennai was anything but easy. I worked multiple jobs. Repairing computers during the day, teaching hardware classes in the evening, and freelancing on weekends. Each role sharpened a different skill, much like how each crop in Thatha's fields served a unique purpose.

The teaching especially changed me. My students at the evening hardware class were mostly young men from villages like mine, first-generation city dwellers trying to find their footing. They reminded me of transplanted seedlings, roots exposed, searching for soil. Some were shy and could barely look me in the eye. Others were brash, covering their fear with bravado. I learned to read each one, noticing who needed encouragement, who needed challenge, who needed space.

One student, Muthu, was particularly memorable. He was from a village near Madurai, the eldest of five children, supporting his family on the three thousand rupees his father earned driving an auto-rickshaw. Muthu's hands would shake when he opened a computer case. He was terrified of breaking something expensive. I paired him with the most complex repair jobs intentionally. "You can't learn to swim by watching the river," I told him. It was a phrase borrowed from Thatha, who had said it about transplanting seedlings in monsoon mud.

Muthu went on to open his own repair shop in Madurai two years later. He called me when he serviced his hundredth customer. I have never been prouder of anyone.

The Marina Night

There were nights of doubt, of course. Moments when I wondered if I had made a mistake leaving home, if I would ever build something meaningful. The loneliest period was my second year. The initial adrenaline of the new city had faded. The novelty of independence had given way to the weight of it. I was sending money home, barely keeping enough for myself, sleeping four or five hours a night between jobs.

One evening I sat on the seawall at Marina Beach, watching the Bay of Bengal churn dark under a hazy moon, and I seriously considered going back to Theni. Not as a temporary visit. For good. I had a plan drafted in my head: I would tell my family I had tried, I had failed, and I was coming home to help Thatha on the farm. The plan felt like a warm bath. Also like drowning.

I called Thatha. I did not tell him I was thinking of coming home. I just said I was tired. He did not give advice. He told me about the farm. What was growing. How the weather had been. How the neighbor's cow had gotten loose and eaten his banana plants. Normal things. Small things. He asked if I was eating well. He asked if my landlord was treating me fairly. He asked whether the new student I had mentioned, the one with the shaky hands, was still coming to class.

"Yes," I said. "Muthu. He's getting better."

"Good," Thatha said. "Good. He needs you."

That was what saved me that night. Not a speech. Not encouragement. The reminder that somebody in Chennai, somebody not on the farm, needed me to be in Chennai. Anchoring is not a dramatic rescue. It is someone reminding you where you come from, quietly, until you remember why you left.

I walked back from Marina to my rented room that night, and I did not go home to Theni.

The Printing Shop

One of the most significant lessons from those early days was the power of small wins. In farming, a single healthy crop can provide seeds for an entire plantation. In business, one satisfied customer can lead to a dozen more.

There was one particular win I will never forget. A small printing company owner came to me with a decade-old computer that kept crashing. His business depended on it. All his clients' designs, all his billing records, everything. The other repair shops had told him to buy a new system. He could not afford one.

I spent an entire Sunday dismantling that machine. The problem turned out to be a swollen capacitor on the motherboard, a tiny thing, barely visible. I replaced it with a capacitor salvaged from a dead power supply in our scrap bin. Total cost to the customer: zero. The machine ran for another three years.

That printing company owner told everyone in his business circle. Within a month, I had more freelance work than I could handle. One zero-rupee repair became the seed for a side business that eventually funded my first real venture.

When I look back at my time in Richie Street, it was not the grand gestures or the big deals that defined my growth. It was the small, consistent actions.

Understanding a customer's real needs. Solving a seemingly minor technical issue. Teaching a single student a useful skill.

The Drumstick Tree

One particular night, after an exhausting shift at a data center where I had taken a second job, I found myself questioning my choices. The weight of sleepless nights and endless responsibilities felt suffocating. I called Thatha, hoping for some clarity.

He shared a story about the drumstick trees on our farm. A strong storm had bent them out of shape years ago, but they continued to bear fruit. They bore more fruit than ever before.

"Sometimes," he said softly, "pressure shapes us into something better."

His words stayed with me. Every hardship became a seed, every struggle a layer of fertile soil. The training program I started for my night-shift colleagues, the freelance repair services I offered to struggling shopkeepers, each initiative grew from necessity, not strategy.

Walking Home

I began to view each challenge as soil preparation. Just as Thatha would carefully prepare the land before sowing seeds, I started laying foundations for the future. Every conversation with a customer, every class I taught, every repair job I completed felt like planting seeds in unknown soil.

Walking through the crowded streets of T. Nagar after a long day, the city often reminded me of our farm back home. The sunset painted the skyline in hues of orange and gold, mirroring the fields during harvest season.

Thatha's words echoed in my mind: "Every field has its season."

Chennai had its own seasons. Seasons of opportunity, of growth, of renewal. But the soil was different here. It demanded adaptability, resilience, and above all, patience.

Breaking new ground is not just about moving to a new place or starting something unfamiliar. It is about learning to read the soil, understanding its needs, and planting seeds with care.

My time in Chennai taught me lessons that no classroom could. The hardware shop on Richie Street was more than a workplace. It was a school. The streets of T. Nagar were more than crowded pathways. They were classrooms. As I reflect on those early days, I realize that every experience, every late-night repair job, every nervous customer interaction, every exhausted walk home, was shaping me.

In breaking new ground, I was not just changing my surroundings. I was changing myself.

Seeds to Plant

Becoming the Seed

When you left home for the first time, what did you pack that turned out to be useless? What did you leave behind that you wish you had brought?

Who is the person in your current life whose success would make you slow down and feel the same steady satisfaction Rajan anna felt that evening? Have you told them they matter?

If you could write an honest account of the one sale, contract, or decision you made early in your career that you still carry uncomfortably, what would it say? You do not have to publish it. Writing it down is enough.

Chapter 3: The Nature of Growth

The corporate world was as different from Thatha's farm as any place I have been. Air-conditioned offices instead of open fields, computer screens instead of crop rows, KPI dashboards instead of the cracked lines in drying soil. And yet, in these gleaming software company offices where I landed my first corporate job, I found myself constantly returning to the lessons I had learned in those quiet fields outside Theni.

I remember calling Thatha during my first month, excited about my position and my salary. He listened quietly, then said something about his tomato plants. "Last season, the plant with the most flowers didn't give the most tomatoes. Watch how you grow, not just how you show."

My first week in that corporate office was disorienting. Everyone wore pressed shirts and spoke in a mixture of English and acronyms I did not understand. KPIs. ROI. Sprint velocity. Scrum master. I sat in meetings and nodded along, furiously scribbling notes that I would look up later at my desk. Imposter syndrome does not begin to describe it. I felt like a farm boy who had wandered into a laboratory. Everything was clean and organized and precise, and I was terrified of touching anything.

Then, about three weeks in, a project hit a wall.

The Shopkeepers' Interface

The team was trying to build a customer management system for small retail shops across Indian cities. They had stuck on the user interface. They had designed something sleek and modern, the kind of interface that would look great in a Silicon Valley demo. But the test users, actual shopkeepers in Chennai's commercial districts, could not figure it out.

I sat quietly in the meeting while senior engineers debated adding a tutorial overlay, simplifying the menu structure, or redesigning the navigation. Then, without planning to, I spoke up.

"Can I talk to the shopkeepers?"

The room went quiet. My manager looked surprised. I was the most junior person there, barely a month in. But he said yes.

I spent two days visiting shops in T. Nagar and Mylapore with a laptop, watching shopkeepers try to use the software. What I saw was exactly what Thatha had taught me about reading soil. The problem was not the shopkeepers' ability. It was our assumptions. We had built the interface the way we thought about data, organized by categories, with menus and sub-menus. But the shopkeepers thought about their business the way they experienced it. Chronologically. What happened today. What is running low. Who owes money. What needs to be ordered.

I spent three more days in those shops. T. Nagar, Mylapore, Nungambakkam. Each neighborhood had its own character, and each shopkeeper had their own way of working. In T. Nagar, I visited Meenakshi's grocery store, where she had been managing inventory with a worn leather notebook for twenty years. She could barely read the code on the keyboard labels, but her fingers moved across the notebook pages with absolute precision. In Mylapore, a young bookstore owner named Rajesh wanted to track customer preferences and sales trends, but had no patience for complex menus. An elderly textile shop owner in Nungambakkam, Kannaiyan, still used a wooden abacus alongside any electronic system. The two sat side by side on his counter like an old marriage that worked.

What struck me across all these shops was how they experienced their business: not as data to be organized, but as events to be recorded. A sequence of moments, not a collection of categories.

I came back and proposed a complete redesign around a daily timeline view. It was so simple it felt almost stupid. But when we tested it, the shopkeepers took to it immediately. "This is just like my notebook," one of them said, "but better." Meenakshi could see at a glance what happened yesterday and what needed attention today. Rajesh could spot customer patterns in the sequence of sales. Kannaiyan pulled out his abacus less and less.

The team's reaction surprised me. The senior engineers were skeptical at first. This was not the modern interface architecture they had been trained to build. But when we showed them the test results, something shifted. One engineer, Vikram, pulled me aside afterward. "I assumed they were the problem," he admitted. "Turns out, we were solving the wrong problem entirely."

That project's success taught me something Thatha already knew: the best seeds will not grow if the soil is not ready. We had been planting advanced-feature seeds in beginner soil.

Reading the Fields I Could Not See

Each role I had held previously had taught me something different about creating value. Computer repair gave me immediate problem-solving. Teaching showed me how to transfer knowledge. Freelancing forced me to manage projects and clients. In the corporate world, I learned about systems and processes, how large teams coordinate across offices and time zones.

Understanding different markets came naturally after years of watching Thatha read his fields. Just as he knew that the soil near the well needed different treatment than the elevated patches, I began to see how different market segments required different approaches. The big enterprise clients were like the deep-soil crops that needed patience and extensive nurturing. Small business solutions were like the quick-yielding vegetables that required less resource but more frequent attention.

I also got my first taste of working across borders. One of our software projects had a small user base in Sri

Lanka and the UAE, and I spent a few afternoons a week on calls with users there, trying to understand how their markets differed from ours. A small retail chain in Colombo had a completely different billing cycle than one in Chennai. A wholesaler in Dubai kept his books in Arabic and in English, simultaneously. What worked for an Indian shopkeeper did not always work for a Sri Lankan one, and assumptions that seemed universal turned out to be extremely local. Thatha's principle — read each handful of soil — turned out to apply to international markets as much as to domestic ones.

Ashok and the Small-Business Product

About eighteen months in, I was assigned to work with a new senior manager, Ashok Reddy, who had come from a much larger tech company in Bengaluru. He was brilliant, but his style was aggressive. All about winning market share, beating competitors, moving fast. In his first week, he wanted to discontinue the small-business software we had built to focus entirely on enterprise clients. The margins were higher. The contracts were bigger. The logic was sound.

I felt something close to panic. That small-business product was not just a revenue line for me. It represented everything I had learned about listening, adapting, and building for real needs. I scheduled a meeting with Ashok, my hands sweating as I walked to his office. I was the junior person. He was the executive.

Instead of arguing why the small-business product was good, I did something Thatha had taught me. I told him a story.

I walked him through the day I had spent in Meenakshi's grocery store. I described her fingers moving across the worn notebook pages, the way her eyes lit up when the software finally worked the way she thought. I told him about the three other shops, each unique, all needing something different.

"That product makes two crore rupees a year," I said, using the Indian numbering convention — a crore is ten million. "The enterprise contracts might make twenty crore. But this product created something else. It taught us how to listen. Every person in our team who worked on that redesign is now better at seeing customer problems instead of just building features."

Ashok was quiet for a long moment. Then he surprised me. "Let's not kill it," he said. "But let's not invest heavily either. Let's keep it because you're right. It's our connection to what real people actually need." He allocated a small team to maintain it while we pursued enterprise contracts.

Within two years, that decision proved prescient. When the enterprise market crashed during an industry downturn, the small-business product was the stable revenue that kept the company afloat. Ashok never said "I told you so," but I would see him smile sometimes when looking at our financial reports.

More importantly, I learned that corporate politics was not something to fear or fight. It was another kind of soil to read. Power dynamics, personal ambitions, company culture. These were all textures I had to understand, just as Thatha read the different layers of earth in his fields.

The Year I Almost Lost My Marriage to Ambition

This part is harder to write. My earlier editions of this book treated the corporate years as a clean arc toward entrepreneurship. The truth is messier.

I had married in my late twenties. My wife — she prefers not to be named in print, so I will call her Nila, a nickname I sometimes use — was a smart, capable woman who had her own career and her own ambitions. We married in the way many South Indian couples of our generation married: arranged introductions, a few supervised meetings, family approval, and then the long unfolding work of actually learning each other after the wedding.

The first years of our marriage coincided with the most intense years of my corporate career. I was building my reputation. I was taking on projects I did not have the bandwidth for. I was traveling, working late, bringing work home. I thought I was investing in our future. Nila experienced it as absence.

There was a stretch, maybe eight or nine months, when I was barely present in my own marriage. I was the successful husband on paper. The husband in the house was someone who ate dinner while reading email, answered her questions without looking up, and fell asleep on the couch at eleven. She did not complain loudly. She went quiet. It took me months to notice the quiet, because I was so busy.

What broke the stretch was not a fight. It was a Sunday morning when I had taken my laptop to a coffee shop to work. She had asked if I could stay home. I had said I needed two hours. Two hours became six. When I came home, she was not angry. She was not anywhere. She had gone to her parents' house for the day, left a small note on the kitchen counter saying so. It was the most polite rebuke in history and it cut me open.

I was not becoming an entrepreneur yet. I was becoming a neglectful husband who was telling himself he was becoming an entrepreneur. Those are different paths and it is dishonest to pretend they are the same.

I share this because I meet too many founders, especially men, who narrate their workaholic years as noble sacrifice. Sometimes they are noble. Sometimes they are just workaholism dressed up as ambition, and the people closest to us pay the price for the costume. I have watched at least a dozen marriages end because a founder confused the two. Mine could have been one of them.

We repaired it. We repaired it by talking, and by me taking an actual vacation for the first time in three years, and by her being more willing to say hard things out loud, and by me being more willing to hear them. But the repair took years, and the marriage would carry that scar for a long time, and it would change what I was willing to do as an entrepreneur later. When founders ask me now whether a given sacrifice is worth making, I ask them who else is paying the bill.

The Decision to Leave

The decision to leave my corporate job came after years of thought, but the final push came unexpectedly. I was nominated for a promotion. A bigger role, more responsibility, better compensation. Everything that looked like success on paper. My parents were thrilled. My wife was relieved that we were securing our financial future. The timing was perfect. Everything was aligned.

And I felt suffocated.

I remember standing in my apartment, looking at the promotion letter, trying to muster excitement and instead feeling a deadness in my chest. When I told Thatha I was considering leaving to start my own business, he did not give me advice about success or failure. Instead, he told me about how he once changed his entire crop pattern because he noticed how some plants grew better in different seasons.

"Sometimes," he said, "you have to trust what you see more than what others tell you."

That year of convincing Nila about leaving a secure job was not easy. She had married a man with a salary, health insurance, and a promising career trajectory. Now that man was talking about opening a biryani shop.

"Are you serious?" she asked one evening as I laid out my loose plan. She was not angry. She was trying to understand, searching my face for signs that I was joking.

I did not have a good answer. I just knew that the corporate walls were closing in, that I was building someone else's vision with the energy I should have been spending on my own. I knew it the way Thatha knew rain was coming, not from the forecast but from the way the air felt against his skin.

The practical conversations were harder than the ideological ones. "We have a mortgage," she reminded me. "My parents helped with the down payment. What happens when the biryani shop doesn't work?"

I had no answer for that. The truth was that there were real dangers. We could lose money, time, the security we had worked to build. I could not promise success. I could only promise that I would be miserable if I did not try.

We fought. We did not fight with anger. We fought with the kind of quiet desperation that comes from loving someone and seeing them walk toward a cliff. She questioned me not out of doubt in me, but out of fear for us. "A biryani shop, Arun? You don't even cook." She was right. I did not cook. I did not have a business plan. I had a feeling and a direction.

What saved that conversation was a trip home to Theni. We went for a week, and Nila sat with Thatha in the afternoon while I was in town on errands. I never found out what they talked about, and she has never fully told me. Whatever he said, something shifted. When we returned to our apartment in Chennai, she did not give permission, exactly. Permission implies she had the right to stop me, and we both knew I would have gone anyway. What she gave was acceptance. Complicated, anxious, conditional acceptance, but acceptance nonetheless.

During one visit home while I was still working through this decision, I found Thatha transplanting some seedlings. "See these small ones?" he said. "They look weak now, but they're just finding their roots. Once they catch, they'll grow stronger than the ones I didn't transplant." He was talking about plants, but he was also talking about me.

The corporate years had taught me valuable lessons about scale and systems, but they had also showed me what was missing. Just as Thatha understood that some plants needed open skies to flourish, I began to realize that my growth required more space than the corporate structure could provide. The entrepreneur in me was like a sapling pushing against the canopy, seeking its own patch of sun.

The final conversation with my manager was unexpectedly easy. When I told him I was leaving to start a business, he nodded slowly. "I've been wondering when you'd tell me," he said. "You've been here but not here for months." He was kind about my departure. He even gave me a few customers to approach about consulting work, something I had not expected.

As I prepared to leave the corporate world, I remembered how Thatha would prepare a field for a new crop. Clearing the old growth. Turning the soil. Making space for new possibilities.

"Every ending," he would say while clearing his fields, "is just preparation for a new beginning."

The skills I had gathered, from the early days in Richie Street through my corporate experience, were like the different nutrients Thatha would add to his soil. Each experience had enriched the ground from which my own ventures would grow. The time had come to plant my own seeds.

Seeds to Plant

In your current role, what part of yourself are you not using, and what would it cost to start using it?

If you described your closest relationships as fields, which ones have you been over-farming without replenishing? What would "replenishing" actually look like, concretely, this week?

When you imagine telling your own Thatha — or your own grandmother, or your own mentor — about the decision you are currently weighing, what version of that conversation are you avoiding? What makes it hard to have?

PART TWO: CULTIVATING WISDOM

Chapter 4: The Ethics of Growth

In the business world, we often hear phrases like "growth at all costs" and "market penetration" and "winner take all." On my grandfather's farm, I learned a different kind of growth. One that put community before commerce, people before profit. This lesson was never more clear than during one particular harvest season that tested everything I thought I knew about value.

We had a bumper crop of tomatoes that year. The vines were heavy with fruit, and I was excited about the potential profits. The mathematics was simple: we had more tomatoes than anyone else, and even at a lower price, we could make good money. But when we reached the market, we found every other farmer had experienced the same abundance. Prices had crashed to almost nothing.

I remember the scene at the market. Crates and crates of red tomatoes, more than anyone could sell, the air thick with their sweet-sharp smell. Farmers were arguing with wholesalers, voices rising. Some were dumping their produce by the roadside rather than pay for the cart ride home. There was something obscene about it. All that food, all that labor, becoming garbage in the span of a morning.

A business school graduate might have advised selling at a loss to recover some costs. Or perhaps storing the produce until prices improved. But Thatha did something that seemed crazy at the time. He loaded the entire harvest back onto our cart and returned to the village.

"Thatha, what are you doing?" I asked.

He adjusted his dhoti and smiled. "Come, I'll show you something about real value."

What followed was a week where every household in our village ate tomato rice and tomato curry. Even the cows feasted on tomatoes. The village children had tomato-stained fingers and clothes from eating them like apples.

"What's the point of growing food," Thatha said simply, "if it can't feed our own people?"

The Invisible Economy

Something else happened during that week, something I have come to think of as the invisible economy. The web of mutual obligation that holds a community together.

The elderly couple who always shared their festival sweets with us brought us fresh *idlis*, steamed rice cakes, in return. The carpenter whose children enjoyed the tomatoes fixed our broken storage shed without charging money. The schoolteacher who received tomatoes taught me mathematics in the evenings for free. The auto-rickshaw driver who ferried our tomatoes to the far end of the village refused payment for a month of rides to the market.

None of this was spoken. No one kept a ledger. But Thatha kept it all in his head, not as debts to be collected, but as threads in a fabric.

Thatha watched the exchange of goods and services flowing through the village one evening. He said only that the real profit was rarely in what you could count.

This idea is not uniquely Indian. Anthropologists have a name for it: the gift economy. Farmers in rural Japan practice versions of it. So do small ranch communities in Montana, so do fishing villages in coastal Ghana, so do olive-growing hamlets in southern Italy. The specific forms change. The underlying principle does not. When a community invests in each other, not transactionally but habitually, the entire community becomes more resilient to shocks.

I think of it as a kind of insurance policy that no one has to buy, because everyone is paying the premium, every day, in small deposits of generosity.

The Biryani Shop

This lesson fundamentally shaped my approach to business years later. When I opened the biryani shop near the industrial areas of Ambattur, a suburb of Chennai dense with factories, I remembered how Thatha understood that different people had different capacities to pay, but everyone needed to eat.

The biryani shop was my first real venture. A small place, eight tables, tucked between a hardware shop and a cellphone repair stall. I chose the location because I had noticed something during my corporate commutes: the factory workers who poured out of the industrial estate at lunchtime had almost nowhere to eat decent food at a price they could afford. The restaurants served the IT workers. The street stalls were inconsistent. There was a gap.

The shop itself was tiny, barely three hundred square feet, with a kitchen so small you had to turn sideways to move between the stove and the counter. But the smells were magnificent. We made our biryani — a fragrant South Asian rice dish of spiced rice cooked with meat or vegetables, originally from the royal kitchens of the Mughal empire — the traditional way. Each grain of rice kissed by ghee. Cooked slowly with marinated meat or vegetables. The whole thing infused with fried onions and mint and that faint whisper of saffron. When you opened the door at lunchtime, that fragrance hit you like a wave, and it was impossible to walk past without stopping.

Nila had insisted on hiring a proper cook, an elderly man named Venkatesh who had worked in hotels before retiring. At first, she was right to push. I had no idea what I was doing. But Venkatesh took pity on me, teaching me the actual craft. How to get the temperature right. How long to let the biryani steam in its sealed pot. How to judge by smell when it was ready. I learned to listen for the slight sound of sizzle under the lid that meant the rice was catching just right on the bottom. A sound as important as any timer.

Becoming the Seed

The factory workers came in around noon, usually in groups, their hands still dusty from work, their shirts darkened with sweat. I noticed how they would hesitate when looking at the prices, doing mental calculations. So we created a pricing system that let office workers pay full price while factory workers could get the same quality food at lower rates during off-peak hours. Nila thought I was being naive. "You're running a charity, not a business," she said. Maybe she was right, technically. But I kept thinking about Thatha's tomatoes.

There were regular customers whose names I learned. Murugan, who worked in the machining section and always ordered extra onions. Kalyan, who was saving money to bring his family from a village in Andhra Pradesh and would count his coins carefully before ordering. Ravi, who treated the shop like his personal dining room, bringing his friends and lecturing them about quality ingredients in a way that felt like he was promoting us.

What made those meals special was not the biryani alone, though it was good. It was the care. Venkatesh would sometimes slip extra meat into a factory worker's plate, then catch my eye and smile like he was getting away with something. One evening, Kalyan's younger brother came in looking thin and tired. Kalyan had mentioned he was sick. Without any discussion, Venkatesh made him a bowl of milky dal and rice, "to help the stomach," he said, refusing payment. "Feed him again tomorrow, same time," he told Kalyan. "No charge."

The shop's margins were not as high as they could have been. But something interesting happened. The factory workers started bringing their families on weekends, paying full price, happy to do it, because they remembered how we had fed them well when they had less to spend. The office workers began ordering from us for their events. Our customers became our marketers, just as the village had become Thatha's strength during tough seasons. Murugan brought his entire machining team for a celebration when he was promoted. Kalyan's family, once they arrived from Andhra Pradesh, would come every Friday evening. Ravi became our unofficial ambassador, dropping our name into conversations all over the city.

I will be honest: the biryani shop eventually closed. The rent increased. A larger chain opened nearby. The numbers stopped working. But what survived was something more valuable than the business itself. A network of people who trusted me, who had seen me treat them fairly, who would later become customers, investors, advisors, and friends in my future ventures. Murugan's nephew came to work at one of my later tech startups. Kalyan invested in my healthy café years later. Ravi became one of my first mentoring contacts, connecting me with other entrepreneurs in his network. The shop died. The soil it built remained fertile.

The Healthy Café

The healthy café, despite its ultimate closure, taught me more about this principle. We never compromised on ingredient quality even when cheaper alternatives were available. "Like soil," Thatha would say, "trust takes years to build and moments to lose."

The café was born from a genuine passion. After years in tech, I had become fascinated by the connection between food quality and performance. How what we eat affects how we think, how we work, how we lead. I partnered with a nutritionist named Shalini and opened a café that served wholesome, locally sourced meals near a tech park in Taramani, a neighborhood of Chennai that had become, in the 2010s, the city's most concentrated IT corridor.

The food was excellent. I still believe that. We sourced organic produce from farms in the outskirts of Chennai, building relationships with individual farmers much like Thatha had done. Our menu changed with the seasons. Millets in summer. Gourds during monsoon. Root vegetables in winter. We made our own breads, our own chutneys, even ground our own grains for idlis. A single lunch included multiple textures and flavors, designed not just for nutrition but for the actual experience of eating.

Customers who ate with us regularly told us they felt different. More alert. Less sluggish after lunch. Even more patient with their colleagues. We had a young engineer named Arnav who came in every day for two years. His team noticed he was calmer, more creative. He credited our food. A product manager, Divya, told us that eating with us helped her think more clearly. She would make major decisions about her product roadmap in our café, sitting with her notebook and a bowl of millet and vegetables.

But excellence has a price. Our costs were genuinely too high. The tech workers loved our food, but many were not willing to pay 30 percent more than the subsidized cafeteria in their office building. We had built a product for the soil we wished we had, not the soil we actually had.

The realization was painful. Watching month after month as the numbers did not work. As the rent consumed more of our margin. As we faced the choice between closing and compromising on quality.

The last day of the café, I remember sitting at one of our tables after we had locked the door. The space was empty. All the plants we had grown on the balcony already given away to regular customers. Shalini had gone home to process the failure privately. I sat there with a cup of the last batch of filter coffee we had made, the good coffee that we had special-ordered from a small grower in Kodaikanal, a hill station in the mountains above Theni.

Divya came by that evening, unannounced. "I heard," she said simply. She sat with me for an hour without saying much, just being there. Then she asked if we would consider consulting for her team. Helping them redesign their office kitchen and nutrition program. It was not a salvage operation. It was Thatha's principle made real: the soil from a failed crop still nourishes what comes next.

While the café did not survive, the trust we built did. Many of those customers followed us to our next ventures, became our first investors, or connected us with new opportunities. Arnav joined one of my later tech ventures as an early employee. Divya became an advisor and eventually helped us raise our first institutional investment round. The café was a failed crop. It enriched the soil for everything that came after.

The Day I Compromised

I want to write about a moment I am not proud of, because a chapter on ethics that only celebrates my ethical choices is not a chapter on ethics. It is a chapter on public relations.

About three years into my consulting work, I had a client, a mid-sized company in the FMCG — fast-moving consumer goods — sector. They were launching a new product line and had hired me to help with go-to-market strategy. The retainer was meaningful. Not life-changing, but meaningful for a consultant still building his practice.

During our work, I discovered that the product had a claim on its packaging that was, at best, creatively interpreted. Not illegal. Not fraudulent. But a marketing framing that implied a health benefit the ingredients did not really support.

I flagged it. The head of marketing said it had been reviewed by legal and signed off. I pushed a little harder. The CEO scheduled a meeting with me, was polite, and made clear without exactly saying so that my job was the strategy, not the claims. They had hired legal counsel for that.

I stayed on the account. I told myself I was staying to have influence from the inside. I told myself that the claim was a gray area, not a black one. I told myself that if I walked, someone less scrupulous would take my place and the product would launch anyway. Each of these justifications was at least partly true. Taken together, they were a pillow I had stuffed under my conscience so I could sleep.

The product launched. It did fine. No one sued. The consumers who bought it got what most consumers get from that category: a product that was roughly what it seemed, with marketing that was somewhat better than reality. I continued working with the client for another eight months, doing work I was proud of, on strategy that had nothing to do with the packaging.

I never told Thatha about it. He was still alive then, and I think I knew that if I described the situation to him, I would not be able to find a justification he would accept. His simplicity was a mirror I could not face.

The lesson I carry from that year is not that I should have quit the account. I am genuinely not sure whether quitting was the right move. The lesson is that I did not discuss it honestly with the person whose judgment I most trusted. I had arrived at a silent accommodation with myself, and the silence was the wrong part, not the choice. A decision you cannot describe to the people you most respect is a decision that deserves another look.

When I advise founders now, I sometimes share this story, and I notice how quickly their eyes change. They wanted a clean lesson. They were ready to hear that I stood up and refused and walked away and my consulting practice flourished as a reward for my integrity. That is not what happened. What happened is that I made a middling choice I have to live with, and the only dividend of living with it is the sharper clarity I bring to the next such choice.

Kemi and the Agritech Pivot

A few years ago I began mentoring a founder in Lagos, Nigeria, named Kemi. She had built an agritech platform that connected smallholder farmers with input suppliers and buyers, cutting out middlemen who had historically squeezed farmers' margins. The technology worked. The farmers loved it. The buyers grudgingly accepted it.

A large multinational agribusiness approached Kemi with an acquisition offer. It was a serious amount of money. Enough to retire the debt she had taken on, enough to reward her team, enough to vindicate three years of eighteen-hour days. Life-changing money in the Nigerian tech ecosystem, which had historically been underfunded relative to its talent.

The offer came with conditions. The acquirer wanted to fold the platform into their broader supply chain, which would mean integrating their pricing algorithms. Their algorithms optimized for their upstream margins. Kemi's algorithms optimized for fair farmer payouts. These were not the same thing. In many cases they were the opposite thing.

Kemi called me late one night, which for her in Lagos meant mid-morning for me. "I don't want to lose this," she said. "I also don't want to become the thing I built this to replace."

I did not tell her what to do. I asked her two questions. Who would she be a year after taking the offer and watching the farmers' margins compress? And who would she be a year after walking away from the money and continuing the slow work?

She sat with those questions for three days and then declined the offer. A year later, a different acquirer approached with a deal that preserved the farmer-payout architecture, at a lower valuation but with the mission intact. She accepted that one.

What struck me about Kemi's situation was how universal the underlying dilemma was. The specifics — Nigerian smallholders, West African supply chains, a multinational agribusiness — were particular. But the shape of the choice was one I have seen in Bengaluru, Chennai, Jakarta, Nairobi, and Ciudad de México. A mission-driven founder is offered money to compromise the mission. The justification is always that the compromise will allow the mission to scale. The actual outcome usually is not that.

Kemi's farmers kept their margins. Kemi kept her integrity. The money was smaller, but the harvest was real.

The Long Memory of Soil

"The soil remembers," Thatha would say while preparing his fields. "How you treat it this season affects what you can grow in the next." How you treat your customers, employees, and community during tough times determines your business's resilience during good times. The tomato harvest of that village week paid dividends for twenty years. The factory workers of the biryani shop paid dividends I am still collecting. The café closed, but its customer base became the first customers of my next venture.

This is the part of ethics that modern business culture undersells. Ethics is not only about right and wrong. It is also about time horizon. A compromise that looks profitable across a quarter often looks terrible across a decade. A generosity that looks foolish in a month often looks like the wisest investment you ever made when the crisis finally comes.

The modern startup world often portrays business as a battlefield where only the fittest survive. On our small farm in Theni, I learned that true sustainability comes from viewing business as a garden where growth should benefit everyone who tends it. When I review business plans or advise on growth strategies now, I find myself asking questions that would make sense to my grandfather. Are we nourishing the ecosystem that supports us? Are we sharing the fruits of our labor with those who help create it? Are we building something that will remain fertile for generations?

Real success is not just about what you gain. It is about what you give back to the soil that nurtures your growth.

Seeds to Plant

Is there a quiet compromise you have made in your current work that you have not described honestly to yourself? Write it down, privately, without excuses.

Who are the Murugans and Kalyans of your business — the customers, suppliers, or early users who supported you when you had nothing to offer? How are you supporting them now that you have something?

When you imagine your company's obituary being written in twenty years, what is the one sentence about how you treated people that you would want to be true?

Chapter 5: Planting Alongside — On Co-founders and the Companion Crop

The phone rang at 11:47 PM. It was a founder named Deepak. His voice was tight. "Anna," he said — *anna*, older brother, a term of respect for someone somewhat senior — "he's leaving. My co-founder. The best friend I've had since college. He wants to sell the company and I don't. He's given me an ultimatum. Sell or he walks, and he's taking two of our senior engineers with him."

I did not try to fix it on the phone. I asked him to come by the next morning. Then I sat at my desk for a while, looking at the city lights through my office window, thinking about companion planting.

What Thatha Taught Me About Marigolds

On our farm, Thatha planted marigolds. Not in a separate flower bed. Inside the vegetable rows, scattered among tomatoes and chilies and okra. To a stranger's eye, it looked disorganized, like someone had forgotten where the flowers were supposed to go.

"See these?" he said one afternoon, pointing at a cluster of bright orange blooms between the pepper plants. "They're not our main crop. But they keep pests away. They make the soil better for everything else. The vegetables grow stronger because the marigolds are here."

The technique is called companion planting. Indigenous farmers have practiced versions of it in Mexico, in Kenya, in Indonesia, in the American Southwest, for thousands of years. It is not a trick of modern agronomy. It is old wisdom: some plants grow better in each other's company than they do alone.

Human teams are the same. The best co-founding pairs and founding teams I have watched are not copies of each other. They are companions. Their strengths are different. Their weaknesses are offset. Their rhythms complement rather than duplicate. And, crucially, their disagreements are part of what makes the soil rich.

I want to spend this chapter on that topic, because co-founder dynamics and early team dynamics are, in my experience, the single largest predictor of whether a startup survives its first three years. More than the product. More than the market. More than the funding. If the founding team is miscast, the company has to win in spite of itself, and most companies cannot.

The Agreement That Never Gets Signed

Before the legal documents, before the vesting schedules, before the cap table, before any of the formal structures that lawyers will insist on, there is an informal agreement between co-founders that almost no one writes down. Writing it down is one of the most important things founders can do in their first month together.

Here is the agreement, in its simplest form. There are five questions, and you need to answer them out loud, together, before you take anyone's money.

What does success look like for each of us, personally, not for the company? Are we trying to build a lifestyle business that pays us each five hundred thousand a year and stays small, or are we trying to build something that gets acquired for a billion, or are we trying to build something that becomes a generational institution? These three answers require different decisions. If we disagree on this, we will disagree on everything else.

How will we decide when we disagree? Not hypothetically. Concretely. Who has the final call on product? Who has the final call on hiring? What happens when we deadlock on a major decision?

What does "full commitment" mean for each of us? Sixty hours? Eighty hours? Can one of us take Sundays off when the other will not? Is consulting on the side acceptable? Is a board seat at another company acceptable? These are not moral questions. They are alignment questions. Two co-founders can have very different answers and still work together well, as long as each of them knows the other's answer.

Under what conditions will we sell the company? A specific number? A specific buyer? A specific time frame? You need to talk about this on day one, even though it feels premature, because when the offer comes and you have not talked about it, you will discover you have wildly different internal numbers, and one of you will feel betrayed.

What is our protocol if one of us is not pulling their weight? Can we have that conversation directly, or do we need a third party? Is there a process for formally reducing someone's equity if they stop contributing?

These questions sound cold. They sound transactional. Founders I suggest them to sometimes resist, saying "we trust each other, we don't need to write these down."

That is exactly when you need to write them down. Trust is not a substitute for clarity. Trust is what allows you to have the clarifying conversations without them destroying the relationship. When you skip the conversations in the name of trust, you are asking trust to do work it cannot do.

I have watched at least ten co-founding relationships shatter because one of these five questions was not discussed at the beginning. The question always returns. The only choice is whether it returns when the stakes are low, or when they are existential.

Liam and the Three-Headed Founder Team

A founder named Liam, based in Dublin, Ireland, came to me a few years ago. He had started a fintech company with two co-founders. On paper it was a dream team. Three technical co-founders from different backgrounds. Complementary skills. Years of friendship. Strong mission alignment.

Six months in, the company was functional. Eighteen months in, it was falling apart.

The specific issue was that the three of them had never decided how decisions got made. When all three agreed, things flew. When two agreed and one did not, the dissenting co-founder would relitigate the decision in side conversations with the team, slowly eroding the authority of whatever they had decided collectively. When the team saw that decisions could be reopened indefinitely, they stopped trusting any decision, and execution slowed to a crawl.

When Liam described the situation to me, he thought the problem was the dissenting co-founder. I thought the problem was the absent structure. The same behavior in a clear decision-making framework would have been healthy dissent. In the absence of a framework, it was sabotage, even though it was not intended as sabotage.

We spent two weeks working on their operating agreement. Not the legal one. The operating agreement, the how-we-actually-work document. They agreed that one of them would be CEO and have a clear tiebreaker vote on strategic decisions. They agreed that product decisions belonged to a different co-founder, and hiring decisions to a third. They agreed on a specific process for raising strategic objections: you get a full airing in the founders' meeting, and if you are outvoted, you commit fully to the decision in public and do not undermine it in side conversations.

It was painful. One of the co-founders left the company three months later, saying he could not accept the new framework. Liam was devastated at first. Then relieved. Then, slowly, clear-eyed. The company stabilized. The remaining two co-founders hired a senior leader to fill the departed co-founder's role with a defined scope, which turned out to work better than the original three-way partnership ever had.

What I told Liam, after the departure, was something Thatha had shown me with companion planting: not every plant helps every other plant grow. Some combinations are beautiful. Some are actively harmful. The skill is honest observation, not wishful thinking.

Soraya in Dubai

Another founder I have worked with closely, Soraya, is an Iranian-American woman based in Dubai who built a logistics platform serving freight corridors across the Gulf and into East Africa. She came to me with a different kind of co-founder problem. Hers was a problem of asymmetric confidence.

Soraya was the primary operator and sole fundraiser. Her co-founder, a brilliant engineer, preferred to stay deep in the technology and let her handle everything else. On the surface this looked like a perfect division of labor. In practice, it meant that over three years, Soraya had accumulated all the external relationships, all the strategic context, all the board dynamics, while her co-founder had become functionally a senior technologist with a co-founder title.

When a critical board vote came up, Soraya realized with sudden clarity that her co-founder could not meaningfully participate. He did not know the board members. He did not know the capital structure. He did not know what the competitors were doing. She had unintentionally built a company where she held all the non-technical context, and he held none of it.

The first question was whether this had been his choice or hers. The honest answer was both. He had preferred to avoid external work. She had preferred the efficiency of doing it herself. Together they had optimized for short-term speed and had ended up with a structural problem.

The fix took a year. Soraya started including her co-founder in board prep, even though it doubled her workload. She took him on customer calls. She shared her fundraising models and asked for his input, even when she had already decided. Slowly, he built the context he had been missing, not because she handed it to him but because she changed the workflow so he could not avoid absorbing it.

The deeper lesson was about how easy it is for a founding team to drift into a pattern that works day to day but creates long-term fragility. The marigolds have to be tended. A co-founding partnership is not something you set up once; it is something you rebuild, in small ways, every month, for years. The moment you stop investing in it is the moment it starts drifting.

When the Companion Becomes a Competitor

Deepak came by my office the morning after the 11 PM call. His eyes were red. He had not slept.

We spent three hours talking. Not about whether his co-founder was right or wrong. About Deepak himself. What he wanted from the company. Whether he believed the product had more to give. Whether the ultimatum had come out of legitimate strategic disagreement or out of some deeper relational fracture that had been quietly growing for months.

The honest answer was the second one. The strategic disagreement was real. The relational fracture was older. They had stopped talking as friends eighteen months earlier, when pressure from a bad fundraising round had frayed their friendship without either of them acknowledging it. They had gone on running the company together while the personal relationship withered. By the time the ultimatum arrived, the actual question was not sell-or-not. The actual question was: can two people who no longer feel like friends keep running a company together? The honest answer to that was no.

Deepak did not sell. His co-founder did leave, and did take the two engineers with him. The company did not collapse the way everyone feared. Deepak brought in a new co-founder with different skills, the company pivoted to a different market, and it ultimately succeeded in ways the original vision could never have.

The co-founder who left eventually built a different company in an adjacent space. They are not friends again. They exchange brief, polite messages on LinkedIn twice a year.

The most important thing I told Deepak during that three-hour conversation was this. The ultimatum was not the emergency. The emergency was the eighteen months you did not have a real conversation. If you survive this, build a practice of having real conversations every week in your next partnership, even when you do not think you need them. Especially when you do not think you need them.

The Robotics Co-founder I Lost

I have to tell my own version of this story. It belongs here, not later.

Between the biryani shop and the consulting work that eventually became my primary career, I partnered with an engineer named Suresh to build automated cleaning robots for commercial buildings. I have written about the business failure elsewhere in this book. What I have not written about is the partnership failure, which mattered more.

Suresh and I had been friends for years before we founded the company. We had the complementary skills. He was the engineer, I was the operator. We had shared values. We had overlapping social circles. On every metric I could articulate at the time, we were a great co-founding pair.

What we did not have was a shared vision of what success looked like, and we never talked about it directly.

Suresh wanted to build a technical showcase. The robot was the point. The business was a wrapper around the robot. If the business made it possible to continue refining the robot, great. If not, the robot was still the point.

I wanted to build a business. The robot was a means to an end. If a different product configuration served the business better, I was prepared to change the product. I believed, mistakenly, that he felt the same way.

For eighteen months, we operated on this unspoken mismatch. Every strategic decision felt a little harder than it should have. Every pivot conversation felt like it was hitting an invisible wall. Neither of us was being difficult on purpose. We were building two different companies in our heads, pretending they were the same company, and our decisions kept pulling the real company in incompatible directions.

When the business failed, what made the failure worse was that it took our friendship with it, temporarily. We disagreed on whether to shut down or persist. We disagreed on what the lessons were. We disagreed on who should return what to whom. The company was tiny and the disputes were small, and still the relationship buckled under them, because we had never built the muscles for disagreeing well.

We repaired the friendship, eventually, over years. We are friends again now, though we will probably never work together again, and that is the right outcome. The lesson I took from the robotics experience was not that co-founding is dangerous. It was that co-founding with an untested relational muscle is dangerous. You do not know what your partnership can handle until you have disagreed about something real. If you have not disagreed about something real before you start a company together, the first hundred disagreements will be simultaneously about the company and about whether the partnership itself can survive disagreement. That is a lot to handle in your first year.

If I had written that operating agreement with Suresh before we started, the failure of the robot business would still have happened. The friendship would probably have survived better. And the learning, for both of us, would have come faster.

Pooja, the Marigold

Not every member of the early team is a co-founder. Many of the most important people in a young company are not on the cap table at all, or are on it in small ways. They are the marigolds.

Pooja was a customer success manager at one of the companies I advised in its early years. She was not the technical genius. She was not the charismatic salesperson. She was something quieter and more important. She kept the team connected to why their work mattered. In every meeting, she would find a way to bring up a customer story. A founder who was using their product to grow her small design agency. A nonprofit using it to track volunteer hours. A small medical practice that saved two hours a day because of a feature Pooja had pushed the engineers to build.

Before Pooja joined, the engineering team had started to drift into a state I have seen at many technical companies. They were brilliant and getting better. They were also becoming slightly contemptuous of customers, who they saw as constantly asking for things the product already did or demanding features that were beneath the product's elegance. The team's pride in the technology was starting to curdle into disdain for the users.

Pooja did not argue with them. She just kept putting customer stories in front of them. Eventually, the engineers who had been coldest began asking her for more stories. The product got better. The customer stories got better. The engineers started doing customer calls themselves, without being asked, because they wanted to see the stories unfold in real time.

That is a marigold. A person whose primary value is not their individual output but the way they change the soil around them, making every other plant grow stronger. Finding one, hiring one, keeping one is one of the highest-leverage moves a founder can make.

The Founder-Employee Friendship Trap

One pattern that has cost a lot of founders a lot of pain: confusing founder-employee relationships with friendships.

When a company is small, the founders and the early employees often become friends in the truest sense. They eat together, argue together, celebrate together, and sometimes live together. Those friendships are real, and they are one of the reliable pleasures of early-stage work. They are also structurally unstable, because the founders are not peers of the early employees. The founders have unilateral authority to change the early employees' livelihoods.

I have watched founders refuse to have a hard performance conversation with an early employee because "she's my friend." The conversation then happens anyway, months later, worse, and with more damage to the relationship than an honest earlier conversation would have caused. The unspoken choice was never "have the conversation or preserve the friendship." The choice was "have the conversation cleanly now or have it poorly later." Postponing is not a third option. Postponing is the second option with interest.

The same applies in reverse. I have watched early employees nurse resentments for years because they felt a founder had prioritized the company over their friendship, without understanding that the founder's role made that prioritization a professional obligation. "She stopped being my friend when she started being my boss" is a sentence I have heard too many times. The more accurate sentence is usually: "She was always both, and I pretended she was only the first one."

The healthy version of this is to name the tension out loud, early. We are friends and we are also colleagues in an asymmetrical relationship. Sometimes the professional role will win. Sometimes the friendship will be strained by professional decisions. Neither of us will be surprised when it happens, because we will have talked about it before it happens.

How to Plant Alongside

If I had to distill what I have learned from watching hundreds of co-founding teams and early founding groups, it would be these things.

Choose for range, not resemblance. The best co-founding pairs I know do not look alike, think alike, or come from the same background. They share values and disagree productively.

Have the five uncomfortable conversations in the first month. Personal success definitions, decision-making, commitment levels, sale conditions, underperformance protocol. Write down the answers.

Build the muscle of disagreement early. Disagree about small things so you are ready to disagree about large things. A partnership that has never been tested has no known strength.

Treat the companion crop as strategy, not overhead. Your early non-founder hires, especially the ones whose value is social and cultural rather than productive, are more important than most founders realize.

Revisit the partnership deliberately. Once a quarter, at minimum, sit with your co-founder and talk about the partnership itself. Not the product. Not the strategy. The relationship. What is working? What is drifting? What do we need to name?

And, finally: if the partnership is broken beyond repair, fix it cleanly or end it cleanly. A long slow decay is worse than either surgery or sunset.

Seeds to Plant

Of the five uncomfortable conversations described earlier, which one have you most avoided with your current co-founder or business partner? What would it cost to have it this week?

Who is the marigold in your current team — the person whose value is social or cultural rather than narrowly productive? Have you told them you see it? Are you compensating them in a way that reflects what they are worth to the ecosystem, not just to their job description?

If you could redo the first month of your current partnership, what would you talk about that you did not talk about the first time?

Chapter 6: The Hidden Seeds

In farming, Thatha taught me, the real work happens before any seed touches the soil. He would spend hours examining a handful of earth, rubbing it between his fingers, feeling its texture, checking its scent. "A good farmer," he said, "reads the soil before reading the almanac."

One morning stands out in my memory. The village almanac had marked it as an auspicious day for planting, and other farmers were busy preparing their fields. But Thatha stood quietly at the edge of our land, watching the early light play across the soil. I was impatient to start. He held up his hand, asking me to wait.

"Look," he said, pointing to subtle signs I had missed. The unusual dryness in the deeper soil. The way certain weeds were growing. The behavior of local birds. "Sometimes, what's not there tells you more than what is." We did not plant that day, and sure enough, an unexpected dry spell followed. While others struggled with withering saplings, our soil stayed ready for when true planting time came.

I have thought about that morning hundreds of times. The ability to see what is not there — the absent signal, the missing data point, the dog that did not bark — is perhaps the most valuable skill I have developed as a mentor and advisor. It is the skill that separates experienced founders from first-timers, veteran investors from newcomers.

This chapter is about hidden seeds. Patterns in markets, in teams, in customer behavior, and in founders themselves that will become load-bearing later, but are barely visible now. If you can learn to see them early, you get years of advantage. If you cannot, you will feel permanently surprised by events that were knowable in advance.

The Founder With No Competition

Recently, a young founder came to me with an impressive pitch deck. His numbers were clean. His projections compelling. His slides well-designed.

"We have no competition," he declared proudly.

I smiled, remembering how Thatha once taught me about weeds: "Every plant has competition. If you don't see it, you're not looking hard enough."

Just as Thatha would examine not just the soil but the surrounding plants, wind patterns, and insect activity, I asked this founder about indirect competitors. About alternative solutions. About changing customer behaviors. His initial confidence gave way to deeper understanding.

"I never thought about it that way," he admitted. "These aren't competitors in our space, but they're competing for the same customer resources."

We spent the next three hours mapping what I call the ecosystem around the ecosystem. Not just who sells similar products, but who else gets a share of his customers' attention, time, and money. By the end, his "no competition" slide had been replaced by a much more honest — and much more compelling — competitive landscape analysis. Investors, I have found, trust founders who understand their threats far more than founders who claim to have none.

When a founder tells me they have no competition, I hear one of three things. Either they are early in thinking, which is fixable. Or they do not understand their market, which is a bigger problem. Or they are consciously minimizing to project confidence, which is the worst case, because it means they will keep minimizing in other contexts, and the hidden seeds will multiply.

ConnectLocal and the Ants Changing Paths

I remember Thatha pointing out how ants would suddenly change their paths days before rain. How certain flowers would close early when storms were approaching. "Nature speaks in whispers," he said, "before it shouts."

This wisdom proved invaluable when I was advising a startup during the early days of the mobile revolution in India. The company, called ConnectLocal, had built a marketplace app for local services. Plumbers. Electricians. Painters. It was working reasonably well on feature phones and early smartphones, with users finding and booking services through simple text-based listings.

I was brought in to advise when they were trying to decide their next focus. Should they expand to more cities? Build more features? Invest in mobile-first design as smartphones became more capable?

Instead of looking at what their users were doing, I suggested we look at what their users were not doing. I spent three weeks watching how people actually used their app. What I noticed was fascinating. The younger users, people under twenty-five, were using the app differently than older users. They were uploading photos of the work they needed done. They were sending WhatsApp messages to service providers even though the app had a built-in chat. They were creating group conversations with multiple providers instead of booking one at a time.

These behaviors seemed inefficient. Why use WhatsApp when we have in-app chat? Why upload photos when text descriptions were faster? But I realized these were ants changing their paths. The younger users were not using the app the way we designed it because they preferred a different kind of interaction. They wanted to see proof of work through photos. They wanted to reach service providers on platforms they already used. They wanted to compare multiple quotes in a group before deciding.

I suggested the company pivot completely. Stop trying to be a booking platform. Become a photo-based recommendation engine. Let users upload photos of their problem. Let multiple service providers respond with solutions. Let it all happen on WhatsApp instead of trying to build a proprietary communication layer.

The CEO was skeptical at first. It felt like admitting their app had failed. But we did a small pilot, and the results were dramatic. Conversion rates increased significantly. User retention improved. And when smartphones became truly powerful devices capable of handling photos and video, this company was already positioned to be a photo-first service platform. By the time the visual-first revolution arrived in earnest, ConnectLocal was already operating in that world. Their competitors, who had stuck with text-based interfaces, suddenly had to rebuild everything.

The key was not special foresight on my part. It was watching for the ants changing their paths, before the storm arrived and made the path change obvious.

When I advise founders on predicting market shifts, I do not tell them to study trend reports or analyst predictions. I tell them to watch their users. Not what users say they want. What they are actually doing. When do they deviate from your intended flow? When do they use your product in ways you did not design for? When do they start using other tools alongside yours?

These are the whispers before the shout.

Elena and the Abandoned Competitor

A founder I mentor named Elena, based in Berlin, built a SaaS product for small and medium businesses in the creative industries. When we first spoke, her market segment already had two well-funded incumbents. One had raised a large Series B; the other had a dominant position in the German-speaking market. Elena's company was a scrappy upstart trying to differentiate on design-led workflow.

What Elena noticed, almost by accident, was something none of the industry analysts were writing about. Users of the Series B incumbent were quietly leaving. Not in big public waves, not in enough numbers to show up in third-party data sets, but in a specific and observable pattern: they were signing up for free trials of three or four alternative products, posting complaints in niche Slack groups, and gradually shifting core workflows to whichever alternative happened to match their specific needs best.

None of this showed up on any market report. Elena only noticed because she was obsessive about reading the community forums and Slack groups her target users actually hung out in, and she kept notes over time.

She made a decision I thought was brave at the time and in retrospect was obviously correct. She moved aggressively to court users of the incumbent specifically, with a migration tool, migration credits, and content that explicitly addressed the pain points she had seen in the forums. She did this before any other competitor had noticed the pattern. Six months later, when the incumbent issued a press release about a pricing change that accelerated the exodus, Elena was already positioned as the natural destination for the defectors. Her growth compounded.

What I took from Elena's story is that hidden seeds often live in information channels that do not show up in traditional market research. Slack communities. Discord servers. Reddit threads. Review sites with fifty reviewers. If you are only looking at paid research, you are looking where everyone is looking. The edge is in the unpaid, unstructured, long-tail sources, and in the patience to read them for years before they pay off.

The Wrong Rockstar

The most painful lessons often come from hiring. What I call planting the wrong seed in the wrong season.

I watched a startup nearly collapse after hiring a "rockstar" VP of Sales from a large tech company. On paper, it looked perfect — like buying premium seeds. But the best sapling will not survive if planted in the wrong season.

This VP, used to managing large teams and wielding big budgets, was like a water-hungry crop planted in dry soil. The startup needed someone who could thrive with limited resources, who could adapt to scarcity. They had hired for the company they wanted to be, not the company they were.

I have seen this mistake repeated so many times that I have developed a simple test for startup hires. Can this person build the thing, or can they only manage the thing once it is built? In a ten-person startup, you need builders. The managers can come later. A senior executive from a large company is like Thatha's premium seeds. They may be objectively superior, but they need conditions that a startup simply cannot provide. The irrigation. The soil depth. The established root network. Without those, the premium seed dies while the hardy local variety thrives.

There is a related hidden seed here, which is the reputation trap. Senior executives from well-known companies arrive with strong brand gravity. The first four months feel like progress because the founders are finally getting taken seriously by investors, partners, and recruits who know the big company name. The actual output is modest, but the social capital feels immense. Founders often fail to notice that the social capital is arriving without the substance, and they give the new hire more scope and more time than their actual performance warrants. By the time the substance has to arrive, six more months have passed, and the company has drifted from its operating tempo. The fix is always painful.

The Founders Who Never Argued

One pattern I learned to recognize early is the hidden seed of co-founder trouble. I have watched brilliant founding teams collapse not because they disagreed, but because they agreed too easily. Or worse, they agreed in public but disagreed in private.

A startup came to me where the two founders seemed perfect. Complementary skills. Shared vision. Clear division of labor. But I noticed something in their interactions. They never challenged each other in meetings. When one spoke, the other nodded. When they discussed strategy, they presented a unified front.

"Tell me about your last disagreement," I asked them.

They looked confused. "Last month?" "Last week?" "Last year?" Nothing. No disagreement at all.

This is a hidden seed of disaster. Founders who never argue are either not listening to each other, or they are afraid to truly speak. Either way, it means real problems are being buried underground, where they will grow silently until suddenly the relationship collapses.

I shared with them a story about Thatha's neighbors. They agreed on everything about farming. They did all the same things at the same times. One year a disease swept through their fields, and both lost everything. Thatha's fields, because my father and he argued about when to plant and how to rotate crops, had variation. When the disease came, it affected us less.

Variation is a feature. Agreement is a bug, when the agreement is purchased by suppression.

The founders started having real conversations after that. Hard ones. One felt pressured by the other's aggressive growth targets. One was worried about product quality while the other prioritized speed. None of these issues were insurmountable. They needed to be surfaced and solved together, not buried and ignored.

The Fraud in the Founder's Chair

Perhaps the most important hidden seed I look for is what I will call unreflected-upon internal chaos. Founders who are managing a personal storm that they have not named.

A founder called late at night, voice breaking, admitting his fears and uncertainties. His name was Akhil, and he had left a comfortable research position at a university to build a software platform that was genuinely transforming how hospitals managed patient records. The product was brilliant. Within six months of launch, they had five hospital systems interested. Within a year, they had contracts worth two million dollars annually.

But Akhil was dissolving under the weight of it. The investors wanted him to hire a CEO. The board wanted quarterly revenue targets. The hospitals wanted customizations. The team wanted clarity. Everyone wanted something, and Akhil found himself in meetings all day instead of building.

"Everyone thinks I know what I'm doing," he said. "I'm making it up as I go."

I asked him what he missed most.

"The research," he said immediately. "Just sitting with the problem, trying to understand it. Not explaining it to investors or defending it to a board. Just thinking."

I shared with him what Thatha once told me during a difficult season: "A farmer who thinks he has mastered the land has forgotten that the land is the master." Great farmers do not lose themselves when the harvest comes. They delegate the business of selling, but they never stop walking the fields.

"Hire someone to do the CEO work," I told him. "Not someone who runs the company without you. Someone who runs the business operations so you can still run the product. You need to be the researcher who occasionally talks to investors, not the CEO who occasionally touches the product."

He was resistant at first. "That feels like a demotion. If I'm not CEO, what am I?"

"You're what you've always been," I said. "The founder. The person who saw the problem. The person who will solve the hard problems no one else can see."

Akhil found the right person. A former operations manager from a medical device company named Shruti who understood both the business and the mission. What made Shruti special was not her operational skill, though she had that. It was her genuine passion for the problem. She had seen poor hospital workflows cause her own mother medical harm, so she understood why Akhil was obsessed with the product.

With that structure, Akhil could spend three days a week on product and research, designing new features based on hospitals' actual pain points. Shruti handled board meetings, investor relations, hiring, and strategy. Within a year, the company had grown meaningfully and was in talks with many more hospital systems.

The operations person made better business decisions because she understood the product deeply, and Akhil made better product decisions because he was not burned out. More importantly, Akhil found his joy again. One day I ran into him at a coffee shop near his office, and he was animated in a way he had not been during those exhausting CEO days.

The hidden seed I had spotted was not the operational chaos. That was visible. The hidden seed was that Akhil was being pulled out of the part of himself that had created the company in the first place. If he continued that trajectory, the product would decline, the mission would hollow out, and the company would become a successful-looking shell. By the time that became visible in the metrics, the damage would be done.

Founders who are out of integrity with their deep nature often do not know it. The metrics can look fine for a long time. The hidden seed is the drift. Spot it early, or pay for it later.

The Time I Missed the Hidden Seed

I am going to break my own storytelling pattern here and tell you about a founder I failed.

Her name, for this book, is Rhea. She came to me three years ago with a marketing analytics company that was growing fast. She was clearly brilliant. The team loved her. Revenue was accelerating. Investors were circling.

What I noticed, but did not say anything about, was that she looked exhausted even when she was telling good news. Her shoulders stayed tense even when she laughed. She described decisions in a tone that sounded more like performance than conviction. In several meetings she referenced her husband's work travel in a way that suggested he had been gone more than usual for a long time. She mentioned, once, that she had not seen her parents in over a year.

I saw all of these. I noted them. I did not bring them up, because I thought my job was to advise her on the business, and she had not asked me to advise her on her life.

Nine months later, Rhea stepped down from her own company. The stated reason was strategic. The real reason was that she had hit a personal breaking point. The company continued without her, got acquired at a decent outcome, and she is now fine and doing other good work. This is not a catastrophic story.

But I still think about it. I think about the month I should have said, "How are you actually doing? Not the company. You."

The hidden seed I missed was not in the business. The business was thriving. The hidden seed was in the founder, and I had reduced my role to the business when the founder was the entire story.

I do not know that my saying something earlier would have changed the outcome. It might not have. But I would have made it clear I saw her as a person, not as a set of company metrics, and that itself would have mattered.

The lesson I carry from that story, and that I now apply to every founder I advise, is that my job is the founder, not the company. The company is downstream of the founder. If the founder is fragmenting and the advisor is still doing strategy sessions, the advisor has misread the field.

The True Skill

The true skill is not in seeing problems. Anyone can spot a withering plant. The art lies in seeing potential problems while they are still seeds, and, more importantly, recognizing opportunities that others miss. Like how Thatha could spot which wild plants indicated rich soil beneath, I learned to recognize signs of fertile ground for innovation and growth.

In today's data-driven world, we often forget that numbers tell us what has happened, not what is about to happen. The hidden seeds live outside the dashboards. In the forum threads. In the tension in a founder's shoulders. In the three users who keep trying to use your product sideways. In the absence of disagreement between people who should be disagreeing. In the competitor's users who are quietly signing up for alternatives. In the founder who mentions her parents once, in passing.

Learn to see those, and you will have years of advantage over anyone else in your field.

Seeds to Plant

What is one customer behavior or user action that you do not currently understand, but have noticed keeps happening? What would it take to investigate it this week?

Is there a founder or colleague whose life you have been reducing to their metrics? What would it look like to ask them a real question about themselves, not their company?

What is the last truly honest disagreement you had with your co-founder, your lead investor, or your most senior team member? If you cannot remember, that is information.

Chapter 7: The Weight of the Seeds

Last night, as I was wrapping up a long day of mentoring sessions, my phone rang. It was 11 PM, and a founder's voice cracked as he spoke.

"Anna, everyone thinks I've got it all figured out. My team looks to me for answers. Investors expect growth. My family thinks I'm successful. But the truth? I'm terrified every morning."

His words took me back to a monsoon evening years ago, when I found Thatha sitting alone on our thinnai, unusually quiet. The rain had been delayed that year, and he had just taken a loan to dig a new well. "Sometimes," he confided, "the hardest part isn't the work itself, but carrying the weight of everyone's hopes."

That evening taught me something profound about leadership. Thatha was not just a farmer tending crops. He was carrying the responsibility for five families who depended on our farm for their livelihood. Just as the young founder was not just building a company. He was carrying the dreams of his team, the trust of his investors, the hopes of his family.

I remember watching Thatha during that delayed monsoon season. Every morning, he walked the fields with the same careful attention, checking the soil moisture, adjusting irrigation channels, making sure every plant received what little water we had. His workers never saw his midnight worries. They only saw his steady presence each dawn.

"The crops don't care if you're worried," he told me one evening. "They only care if they're tended."

This chapter is about that specific weight. The weight founders carry that other kinds of workers do not. It is the weight of holding things together in public while coming apart in private, of projecting steady confidence that you do not feel, of being responsible for outcomes you cannot control and people whose lives depend on your decisions.

If you are a founder reading this, I want you to know, early and plainly: the weight is real. The people telling you it is just stress, or that you should sleep more, or that you should take a vacation, are not wrong, but they are not quite right either. Founder weight is a particular shape. It deserves its own treatment.

The Founder Who Stared at the Burn Rate at 4 AM

One founder I worked with had not slept properly in weeks but maintained an energetic presence in team meetings. Like Thatha, who would wake up at 4 AM during difficult seasons, she used the quiet hours before dawn. But she was using them wrong.

"What do you do at 4 AM when you can't sleep?" I asked her.

"I look at our burn rate spreadsheet," she said.

"Stop doing that," I told her. "At 4 AM, the spreadsheet only tells you one thing. That you're going to die. Instead, at 4 AM, write down one thing you're grateful for about your company. One customer success story. One team member who surprised you. Then go back to sleep. Look at the spreadsheet at 10 AM, when you can actually do something about it."

This is a small thing. It is also a real thing. The 4 AM mind is not the 10 AM mind. Decisions made at 4 AM are almost always worse than the same decisions made at 10 AM. Time-shifting your dread by six hours is not a productivity hack. It is a survival protocol.

There is a broader principle here. The founder's job requires a kind of regulated optimism. Not false optimism. Not denial. A disciplined practice of not letting the darkest moments of the day govern the weightiest decisions. Thatha had a version of this. He did not pretend the fields were green when they were brown. But he did his planning in the morning, before the heat of the day. He did his worrying in the evening, in private, with a cup of coffee and a slow cigarette. He did not mix the two.

Ravi and the Layoffs

One founder came to me struggling with layoffs, his first ever. Ravi's tech startup had burned through funding faster than projected. They had hired aggressively when the investors assured them more money was coming. The money did not come. Now, eighteen months in with a team of twenty-five, he had to let go of eight people.

He came to my office looking like he had not slept in days. His hands were shaking.

"I hired them," he said. "I looked them in the eye and told them they were building something amazing. Now I'm firing them." His voice broke on the word "firing."

I did not try to make him feel better. I told him about Thatha and a particularly difficult drought year. We had hired extra workers to dig deeper wells, and for a while it seemed like the right decision. But as the water levels kept dropping, it became clear we could not maintain wages for everyone.

Thatha did not hide it. He did not give sudden notice. He called a meeting with the workers weeks in advance. He was honest about what was happening. And then — this is the part that always struck me — he did not just dismiss them. He spoke to other farmers first, securing positions for them. He wrote recommendations. He helped one worker start his own small vegetable stall, lending him seeds from our stores.

"When you have to reduce the weight of the cart," Thatha said later, "make sure what falls off has somewhere soft to land."

Ravi took this to heart. He did not just send termination notices. Over the course of a week, he scheduled individual conversations with each person. In those conversations, he was honest about why it was happening. He apologized for the position he had put them in. And then he acted.

He reached out to his network of investors, mentors, and other founders. He found roles for five of the eight people within two weeks. For the other three, he paid an extra month's salary from his own savings and gave them time and support to find their next opportunity. He wrote detailed, honest reference letters for everyone. He stayed in touch, checking in monthly to see how they were doing.

The team that remained — the seventeen people who kept their jobs — did not feel relieved. They felt honored. They had seen how their leader treated people even in the worst moment the company had faced. They had seen that Ravi had put his own financial burden on himself rather than dump it on others.

The company survived. Ravi's transparent handling of those layoffs became part of the company's DNA. When the next crisis came — and there was one, eighteen months later — the team did not panic. They had already seen how Ravi handled hardship.

The Loneliness of Leadership

During one particularly vulnerable mentoring session, a founder asked me how I deal with the loneliness of it all. I shared what Thatha once told me during a failed crop season: "The same sun that dries your fields also helps you find your way." The challenges that isolate us also shape us into better leaders.

But carrying this weight alone is unnecessary. Just as farmers in our village had systems of mutual support during difficult seasons, founders can build their own support systems.

The peer network emerged naturally in our village, like how Thatha would meet with other farmers under the banyan tree, sharing concerns they could not express to their workers. These were not formal meetings, but they were crucial for survival. Today, I help founders create similar circles of trust. Spaces where they can be vulnerable with others who understand their journey.

I facilitated one such group for three years. Six founders, meeting monthly at a quiet restaurant in Adyar, a residential neighborhood of Chennai. No phones on the table. No investors or employees present. What was said in the room stayed in the room. The conversations that happened over those dinners saved at least two of those companies. Not through advice. Through the simple act of being heard by people who understood.

The peer network taught me something crucial about the specific burden of founders. It is not just that the work is hard. Many jobs are hard. It is that founders carry a unique combination of burdens. They are responsible for the vision but do not control the outcome. They make decisions that affect families but cannot predict the market. They project confidence while managing doubt. They inspire while acknowledging fear.

In the peer network, we created space for all of it. One evening, a founder from an HR tech company called in. He was in a hospital waiting room after his father had a stroke. He kept apologizing for having to leave early, worried about letting the group down.

"Your father had a stroke," another founder said quietly. "If you left the group right now forever, that would be the right choice."

He stayed for two more hours, finding comfort in telling his peers about his fear that his father would not recover, and his other fear that he might lose his company while dealing with it. No one tried to solve either problem. They sat with him in both.

That kind of container is rare in a founder's life. Boards want optimism. Investors want confidence. Employees want certainty. Family wants reassurance. The peer network was the one place where a founder could say, "I don't know if we'll make it. I don't know if I made the right choices. I'm terrified." And the response was not advice. It was: "I know. I feel it too. And you're going to keep going anyway."

Prerna and the Marriage Market

One of those founders was Prerna, a first-generation entrepreneur whose traditional family could not understand why she had left a stable job. Her father, a retired government servant, would ask at family dinners when she was going to get "a real job." Her mother worried constantly about her marriage prospects — in many Indian communities, an unmarried woman in her thirties generates significant family anxiety — and would say things like, "What girl will reject a successful founder-son, but what family will accept a founder-daughter who hasn't made it yet?"

Those questions followed Prerna home after long, exhausting days of building.

The founder meetings became her lifeline, not because I gave advice but because the other founders got it. When she mentioned that her father had called after reading that another startup in her space had raised funding, asking why her company did not have investors yet, another founder in the group said quietly, "My parents introduced me to three different marriage prospects last month." And just like that, the burden got a little lighter by being shared.

Six months later, Prerna's company hit an inflection point. Revenue tripled. An investor came through. And she brought her parents to her company's office for a tour. Her father met some of her employees, saw the technology they had built. After the tour, he told her quietly, "I didn't understand this before. I thought you were being reckless. I see now that you were building something."

What struck me about Prerna's arc was the cultural specificity of her weight. She was not carrying the same weight as a male founder in her cohort. She was carrying her own entrepreneurial burden plus the ambient disapproval of a community that had a very particular vision of what her life should look like. Founders from underrepresented groups in their industries — women in male-dominated sectors, minorities in homogeneous venture markets, first-generation immigrants whose families want stability rather than risk — carry that second weight whether or not anyone names it. Peer networks that include people who understand that specific second weight are disproportionately valuable. Generic advice can mislead. Specific witness does not.

When I tell founders now about peer networks, I am careful to say: the right peer network for you is not a generic founder group. It is specific to the particular shape of the weight you are carrying. Founders carrying a second weight on top of the founder weight — women in male-dominated sectors, minorities in homogeneous markets, first-generation immigrants, founders in geographies far from their families — usually need more than one circle. The generic founder group will hold the generic founder weight. The second weight needs its own witness. Build the second circle deliberately. Do not assume one room can hold both things.

Thatha's Own Silence

I have made Thatha sound, so far in this chapter, like a man who handled the weight of his farm with calm equanimity. That is mostly true. It is not fully true.

Thatha had an elder brother named Paramasivam, who died young. After that death, Thatha married his brother's widow — my grandmother, Seeniammal — and raised his brother's two children, my father Rajiah and my aunt Mariammal, as his own. The farm he worked, the family he fed, the name he gave the children — none of it had begun as his. He made it his, quietly, without ceremony, for the rest of his life. He did not speak of his brother. He did not speak of what it cost to take on another man's life as his own. That was the code he lived inside: carry it, don't name it.

I share this because it changes how you should read the rest of this chapter. When I have written about Thatha's steadiness, the weight he carried, his refusal to perform either his wins or his losses — I have been describing a man whose entire adult life was an exercise in carrying a responsibility that was not originally his, and doing it without remark. That steadiness had a shadow behind it. The external calm is worth emulating. The internal silence is not.

The founders I have watched collapse most badly were the ones who copied the external poise of their mentors without developing anywhere to put the internal weight. If you are going to borrow Thatha's steadiness, borrow it without borrowing his silence. The carrying is the real work. Pretending it costs nothing is not a lesson. It is a trap.

The Founder Who Could Not Come Back

I will not tell this story in detail, out of respect for the people involved. I will tell you only that one of the founders I mentored in my early years burned out so badly that he had to step away from his company, and then from work entirely, and then from his marriage. He did not come back in any of those senses for years. He is well now. But the road was longer and darker than any of us, including him, anticipated.

What I learned from watching that happen, and being unable to help as much as I wanted, is that founder burnout is not a tiredness that a vacation fixes. It is a systems failure that compounds over years. By the time it becomes visible, a lot of damage has already happened, and the recovery is not a week off. The recovery is a rebuild.

If you are reading this and recognizing yourself, please hear me. You are not weak. You are not failing. You are responding normally to a sustained abnormal load, and the load is the problem, not you. Get help. Talk to someone who has walked this before. Take the rest before you are forced to take it. The rest you choose is always shorter than the rest you are forced into.

Thatha's Sunrise Rule

One founder I work with recently implemented what I call Thatha's Sunrise Rule. The first hour of each day is for walking the fields. No email. No Slack. No meetings. Not even the burn rate spreadsheet. Just observing, without immediately acting.

Like Thatha's pre-dawn field inspections, this practice helps her separate the signal from the noise, the urgent from the important. After two months of the rule, she told me the quality of her decisions had noticeably improved. The hour had not reduced her output. It had relocated it from reactive mode into reflective mode, and the same eight hours of work produced better results.

The most powerful lesson about carrying weight came from watching how Thatha transplanted saplings. He taught me to grasp them firmly enough to ensure they stayed together, but gently enough that I did not crush them.

"Leadership," I tell founders now, "is like that. Being strong enough to hold things together, but gentle enough not to break what you're trying to grow."

The branch that bears the most fruit always bends the lowest. That is the founder you are becoming, whether you wanted to or not.

Your doubts do not make you weak. They make you human. Your fears do not make you less of a leader. They make you a more empathetic one.

Seeds to Plant

What is your 4 AM mind telling you, and what would it cost to stop listening to it at 4 AM?

Who is in your peer circle of witness, specifically the people who understand your particular shape of weight? If that circle does not exist yet, who might be in it, and what would it take to assemble it this quarter?

Is there a silent grief, or a silent worry, that you have been carrying the way Thatha carried his brother's death? What would it cost to name it to one trusted person this month?

Chapter 8: Reading the Weather

On Money, Investors, and the Storm Seasons

🌱 🌱 🌱

There is a memory I carry from the years before I knew anything about money.

It is late May in our village. The pre-monsoon air has that particular weight — heavy, still, not yet released. Thatha is standing barefoot in the yard, looking at the sky. He is not looking at clouds. He is looking at the way the leaves of the neem tree are turning their pale undersides up. He is watching a line of small black ants moving in a hurry along the compound wall. He is feeling the pressure on his skin.

He says, almost to himself, "Mazhai varudhu." The rain is coming.

I am eight or nine. I look up and see only sky. "When?" I ask.

"Three days. Maybe four."

I want to ask how he knows. He must see the question on my face, because he says, without looking down at me: "When you have lived through fifty monsoons, you stop needing the radio."

Three days later, the first heavy rain of the season breaks over our roof, and Thatha is already inside, his tools wrapped, the seed sacks moved from the lower shelf to the upper one, the small drainage channel he had dug around the tomato bed already deepened by another two inches.

For years I thought this was magic. It was not magic. It was attention. He had been reading the weather every day of his life. He could not have told you the names of the signals he was reading. He could only tell you what was coming.

I wish someone had told me, when I started raising money for my businesses, that investors are weather.

My First Raise (and What It Bought Me)

When I started my consulting business after the laptop years, I did it the only way I knew how: with my own savings and a small loan from a cousin who had just sold a piece of land. Eighteen months in, we were profitable. Not richly profitable. Profitable enough to pay three salaries — mine, my partner's, and one administrative assistant who kept us from drowning in invoices.

A friend introduced me to an angel investor visiting from Singapore. He had built and sold a software company a decade earlier. He liked our story. He thought we could grow faster.

He offered us a small cheque — small by his standards, large by ours. About forty lakh rupees, which at the time was around fifty-five thousand US dollars. In exchange, ten percent of the company.

Becoming the Seed

I remember the conversation with my co-founder. We sat in a tiny South Indian breakfast place near our office, eating idli with one hand and arguing with the other.

He wanted to take it. "We can hire two more consultants. We can take that bigger client we've been turning away because we don't have the bench."

I wanted to refuse it. "We're profitable. If we take this money, we're not building a profitable consulting business anymore. We're building something we will then have to sell, or list, or hand to him at some price he is happy with. The clock starts."

We took the money.

I do not regret that decision. The money let us hire faster, take bigger projects, build the brand that eventually let us launch product. But it cost something most founders do not understand until it is too late.

The money did not just buy seats and salaries. It bought a clock.

Before the money, our timeline was: as long as we want. After the money, our timeline was: until our investor wants something to happen. He was a patient man, and a kind one, and he never put a foot wrong with us. But the clock was real. We could feel it in every quarterly review, in every conversation about strategy, in the way we now described our business to others.

Thatha would have called this "kadan" — debt — even though it was equity. To him, anything you took from someone else came with weight. He did not believe in painless capital. The well he dug in 1968 with a loan from the village cooperative shaped every decision he made for the next twenty years. He paid that loan off in eleven years and was a different man for it.

When you take money, understand what you are taking. You are not just taking rupees or dollars or euros. You are taking time, and you are taking voice. Both are finite. Both are precious.

🌱 🌱 🌱

Liam and the Down Round

I have already introduced Liam, the founder in Dublin who built a fintech company with two co-founders he had to renegotiate his way out of. Liam reappears in this chapter for a different reason.

About fourteen months after we resolved his co-founder mess, Liam called me on a Sunday morning.

"Anna," he said — he had picked up the Tamil greeting from me and used it now even though he was Irish — "I think we are about to do a down round."

A down round is when a company raises money at a lower valuation than its previous round. Investors who came in earlier see their stake on paper become worth less. Founders see their ownership diluted further. Employees with options see those options become a less interesting proposition. It is the corporate equivalent of admitting in public that the harvest has been smaller than you promised.

Liam's last round had valued his company at thirty-eight million euros. The new round was being offered at twenty-two million.

"What changed?" I asked.

"Everything and nothing. We hit our revenue numbers. We did not hit our growth rate. The market repriced fintech across the board. Two of our competitors raised at lower valuations last quarter. Our existing investors are pushing for the deal because they would rather own a smaller percentage of a funded company than a larger percentage of one that might not survive."

We talked for two hours. He had three options. He could take the down round and accept the dilution. He could refuse the round and try to extend his runway by cutting deeper into his team. He could try to find new investors at the old valuation and almost certainly fail, burning months of his time.

He took the down round. It was the right decision, but it cost him something I do not think he expected. It cost him the certainty he had felt for two years that the trajectory only goes up. That certainty had been quietly fueling him. When it cracked, he had to find a different fuel.

He found it. The company is fine now — actually growing nicely, having repriced its way into a more honest place. But Liam said something to me a year later that I have repeated to many founders since.

"The down round was not the bad day. The bad day was the day before, when I still believed the story. The down round was the day I had to start telling the truth."

Money rounds are weather. They will turn. The founders who survive are the ones who were ready, who had moved the seed sacks to the upper shelf before the first heavy drop fell.

🌱 🌱 🌱

Soraya and the Patience of Capital

You met Soraya in the chapter on co-founders — the Dubai logistics founder who almost lost her co-founder over an asymmetry of confidence. There is more to her story.

When I first met Soraya, she was being courted by three investors for her Series A. Two were prominent regional VCs. One was a strategic — a large logistics company that wanted both equity and a partnership. Combined, they were offering her around twelve million dollars at a valuation that would have made her, on paper, a wealthy woman at thirty-one years old.

There was just one problem. The terms were aggressive. The strategic investor wanted a board seat, a right of first refusal on any future sale, and exclusivity in three product categories. The two VCs wanted a 1.5x liquidation preference and anti-dilution protection that would have crushed common stock holders — including her early employees — in any down scenario.

I was on a call with her where she was leaning toward taking the deal. "I can fix the relationships later," she said. "Right now I need the money to scale."

I asked her one question. "Soraya, how many months of runway do you have today, with current revenue, no new money?"

She did the math. "Fourteen months."

"And what is your monthly growth rate right now?"

"Twelve percent month over month."

I waited.

"You think I should wait."

"I think you should ask yourself whether the version of your company that exists in fourteen months, growing at twelve percent a month, will be raising on terms it likes better than these terms."

She waited. She raised six months later, at a higher valuation, with cleaner terms, from a different lead investor. The dilution was about half what the original deal would have inflicted. The board seat went to someone aligned with her, not to a strategic with conflicting interests.

That decision — the patience to wait — was worth more to Soraya, in the long run, than the money would have been if she had taken the first deal. Thatha had a phrase for this. "Pazham pazhuga vendum." The fruit must be allowed to ripen. You can pick a mango when it is hard and green and bring it home in your bag, but it will never taste the way it would have if you had let it ripen on the tree.

I tell every founder I work with: do not take money the day you need it. Take it the day before you need it, and never the day after.

🍎 🍎 🍎

Thatha and the Well Loan

There is a loan that shaped our family.

In 1968, Thatha decided we needed our own well. The village had a common well, but it was a long walk and a slow draw, and the politics of who used it when had become tiring. He went to the village cooperative and took a loan of three thousand rupees, which in 1968 was not a small amount of money for a small farmer.

He dug the well himself, with help from two laborers. It took four months. The well hit good water at twenty-eight feet. He installed a hand pump. He came home one evening and washed his face in the new water and called my Patti — my grandmother — out to look at it.

He paid that loan off over eleven years.

For eleven years, Thatha never bought new clothes. Patti made his shirts and his dhotis from cloth she got from a relative who had a small handloom. He drank coffee at home, never in town. When other farmers in the village bought small radios, he did not buy one. When the village had a small festival and the men contributed a few rupees each for the deity's procession, Thatha contributed only the minimum.

He told me once, much later: "I made one decision in 1968. For eleven years, every other decision was made for me by that one decision."

I think about this every time I take money in a business.

The decision to take capital is not a single decision. It is a chain of decisions you have not yet made, each one shaped by the first one. The hire you cannot make. The customer you cannot fire. The pivot you cannot try. The vacation you cannot take. The mistake you cannot afford. The argument with your investor you cannot have.

This is not an argument against taking money. Thatha did not regret the well loan. The well doubled our productive capacity, let us grow vegetables in the dry months, paid for itself many times over. The loan was the right decision.

But it was not a free decision. There is no such thing.

When you take money, sit with the question: am I willing to live the next eleven years inside the consequences of this single choice? If you are, take it. If you are not, do not take it because someone else is excited about your company.

Investor Relationships Are Long Marriages

A claim that will sound exaggerated but is exactly true: an investor relationship is more like a marriage than a transaction.

You will be in this person's life for somewhere between five and twelve years, and probably longer if the company does well. You will share information with them that you share with very few other people. You will see each other at your worst — the worst quarters, the worst hires, the worst public moments. You will need to be able to disagree with them and still trust them. You will need them to be able to be wrong with you and not punish you for it. They will need to be able to push back on you and have you actually hear it.

If those things are not present at the term sheet stage, they will not be present three years in.

I have worked with founders who took money from investors they could not stand because the cheque was the largest one offered. I have not seen this end well. The founder spends an inordinate amount of energy managing the relationship. Quarterly reviews become performance theater. Honest conversations stop happening. The investor becomes the audience the founder is performing for, instead of the partner they are building with.

I had a conversation with a founder named Hannah, in Stockholm, who had taken money from a fund she described to me as "the biggest cheque, but not the right people." Two years in, she was spending what she estimated at twenty percent of her time managing the relationship — preparing for meetings, smoothing over disagreements, anticipating their next concern.

"What would you spend that twenty percent on if you got it back?" I asked her.

"Customers. Product. My own thinking time."

"Then you are not paying twenty percent. You are paying twenty percent plus what you would have built with that twenty percent."

She did not change anything immediately. But she changed the next round. She raised at a slightly lower valuation from a smaller fund whose partner she had grown to trust over a year of casual conversations. She told me, two years later: "It was the best trade I ever made."

Choose your investors the way you would choose a co-founder. The cheque is not the deal. The relationship is the deal.

🌱 🌱 🌱

When to Say No to Money

There are three seasons in a company's life when you should say no to money even on excellent terms.

The first is when you have not yet figured out your business. If you raise before you understand your unit economics, your customer acquisition cost, your retention — the money will let you scale a business that does not work. You will run faster in the wrong direction.

The second is when the money carries terms that will distort your decisions. A high valuation can be a trap. Raise at a hundred million on the hope of becoming a billion-dollar company, then find your honest market is two hundred million, and you cannot exit cleanly. You will chase the billion you do not actually believe in instead of building the great two-hundred-million-dollar business you have.

The third is when the money will pull you away from your values. A founder once told me he had been offered money from a fund whose previous portfolio company had been credibly accused of misleading customers about safety. I asked him whether he wanted to introduce his new investor to his mother. He passed on the money. A year later he told me it was the most expensive decision he had ever made, and he would make it again.

Money is a tool. The wrong tool, even when offered freely, is still the wrong tool.

Unit Economics and the Honest Café Conversation

I keep coming back to my friend with the café in Mylapore. You met him in an earlier chapter — the friend who served tea brewed with cardamom and asked me one Saturday afternoon why his second outlet was losing money.

We sat with his books. We worked through it together. The first café was profitable because his rent was old, his staff was loyal and modestly paid, and he himself was working in it forty hours a week. When he opened the second one, the rent was new and three times as high, the staff was new and had to be paid market rates, and he could not be in two places at once.

The unit economics of the second café did not work. Not because of bad management. Because of the structure.

He could have raised money to open three more cafés on the same model. The money would have made the problem larger, faster. Instead, we worked on the structure. He raised prices in both locations. He cut a slow-moving sandwich from the menu and replaced it with a higher-margin item. He moved the second café to a smaller, cheaper space two streets over. Six months later, both locations were profitable.

He never raised money. He grew, slowly, to four locations. He is happier than most founders I know.

There is a story we tell ourselves in the venture world that scale solves problems. Sometimes it does. Often it does not. Often it makes a small problem into a large one.

Before you raise, ask yourself: are my unit economics good? If they are, capital may help you grow faster. If they are not, capital will only let you lose money faster. A leaking bucket carries less water the bigger you make it.

Run the honest numbers before you ask anyone for money. If you cannot make the numbers honest, do not raise. Fix the numbers first.

Bootstrapping Versus Venture: Different Soils

I have been on both sides. They are different soils, and different things grow in them. Neither is better. They are just different.

A bootstrapped company is a tomato grown in your backyard. You water it. You eat what it produces. It will grow as much as your soil and attention can support, and no more. That is its limit and also its freedom.

A venture-backed company is a commercial farm. You take inputs from outside — capital, expertise, pressure. It can grow much larger and feed many more people, but it has obligations. The investors expect a return. The clock matters. The crop matters more than the gardener.

Some founders are temperamentally suited to the backyard. They want to work at their own pace, answer to no one. For them, the venture path will be a misery even if it makes them wealthier on paper. Some founders are suited to the commercial farm. They are energized by scale. They want to feed many. They will take instructions from the season and the investor in exchange for the chance to grow something larger.

Most do not know which one they are until they have tried both. That is fine. But before you take the venture path, ask yourself: do I want to own this company, or run it for someone else's portfolio? Both are honorable. Only one is what most people imagine when they say "founder."

A Note on Storms

Every founder I have worked with has had at least one storm season. Some have had three or four. Storms are the seasons when nothing works the way you expected it to. Revenue softens. A key hire leaves. A customer churns. A regulator writes a letter. The market reprices your sector. Your investor's fund has a problem of its own. Your co-founder is going through a divorce. Two of these things happen at once, and then a third.

You do not control when the storm comes.

You do control whether you have prepared for it. You control whether your seed sacks are on the upper shelf. You control whether your unit economics are honest. You control whether your investor relationships are real or theatrical. You control whether you have built a small reserve, both financial and personal, that lets you absorb a bad month without panic.

Thatha used to say that the farmer who does not prepare for the bad monsoon is the farmer who has never seen one. The first storm of your founding life will surprise you. The second one should not.

When the storm comes — and it will — the right response is not heroic action. It is patient action. Reduce what you can reduce. Protect what you must protect. Have the honest conversation with your investor before they have it with you. Talk to your team before rumors start. Cut the right things, not the easy things. Wait for the rain to pass.

After the rain, the soil is often better than it was before. But only for the farmers who were still standing.

🍎 🍎 🍎

Seeds to Plant

Three questions before you raise:

What is your honest relationship with money in your business right now — is it a tool you are using, or a story you are telling? When did you last look at your unit economics with a cold eye, and was the picture you saw the same as the picture you describe to others?

If you have raised capital, do you respect the people on your cap table the way you would respect a co-founder? If you have not raised capital, are you avoiding it for the right reasons, or because you are afraid of the conversation? If you took capital tomorrow, on the terms most likely to be offered to you, what would you have to give up — and would you give it up gladly?

When was the last time you said no to money? What did saying no protect?

Becoming the Seed

If a storm hit your company in the next ninety days — a churned customer, a key hire leaving, a market repricing — what would you do in the first week? Have you written it down? Have you talked about it with your co-founder? If not, this might be the week.

Watch the leaves. Watch the ants. Read the weather before you need to.

Chapter 9: Growing Through Seasons

On the Years That Are Not the Spring

There is a season in our village that no one writes poems about.

Everyone writes about the monsoon. The first rain. The smell of wet earth. The miracle of the green coming back. There are songs about it. There are festivals built around it. There are entire genres of Tamil cinema where the hero and heroine fall in love during the first rains.

There is no song about the third week of the second monsoon, when the soil is waterlogged and the seedlings are rotting at the base because the field has not drained properly. There is no song about the long hot weeks of June before the rain comes, when the wells are running low and the cattle are restless and the leaves of the tamarind tree have stopped moving in the wind because there is no wind.

But these are most of the year. The seasons that no one writes about are most of farming. They are most of every business, too.

Founders read books about the breakthrough year. The hockey-stick year. The year the company tripled. They do not read books about the year nothing happened. The year revenue grew nine percent and the team grew two people and you wondered, on a Tuesday morning, whether you should still be doing this at all.

Most years are that year.

This chapter is about those years.

※ ※ ※

Priya and the Logistics of Patience

Priya, the logistics founder you met briefly earlier, runs a B2B logistics company that serves small-to-mid-sized exporters out of Chennai and Tuticorin. She started it nine years ago. She is now running a company that does about eighteen million dollars in revenue, with healthy margins, and she sleeps well at night.

What you do not know about Priya is that years three through five of her company were the years no one wrote about.

In year one, she got her first ten clients. Word of mouth. Easy. In year two, she got to twenty-five clients on the back of a single big customer who recommended her to four others. By year three, the easy referrals had run out. The market she had been serving was small. She had to figure out either how to expand into adjacent customer segments or how to deepen her share of the existing ones.

She tried both. She failed at both for two and a half years.

She spent year three trying to enter the e-commerce fulfillment space. The unit economics were different.

The customers were different. Her existing team did not understand the product. After eighteen months of investment, she shut down the e-commerce vertical with a loss equivalent to about a third of her annual revenue.

She spent year four trying to deepen her share of the export logistics market by signing exclusivity deals with larger exporters. The exporters wanted lower prices in exchange for exclusivity. The lower prices crushed her margins. She gave up on exclusivity by the end of year four.

In year five, she did almost nothing new. She fixed the things that were broken. She rebuilt her operations process. She replaced two hires that had not worked out. She had a long, honest conversation with her one remaining co-founder about what they were actually trying to build.

She told me later: "Year five was the year I stopped trying to grow and started trying to be excellent."

Year six grew thirty-eight percent. Year seven grew forty-one percent. Year eight grew thirty percent. The growth came not from a new strategy but from the fact that her base business was now dramatically better than her competitors' base business. Customers who had churned in year three were coming back in year seven, telling her: "You are different now."

She had not changed her market. She had not changed her product category. She had simply gotten very good at the thing she had been mediocre at for five years.

I tell new founders Priya's story whenever they are in their year three or year four and panicking. Most companies do not grow up. They grow sideways for a long time, and then they grow up suddenly when the sideways years finally compound into excellence. The sideways years are not failure. They are the soil being prepared.

There is a saying about idli batter — wait until it rises on its own. You can pour it into the steamer when it is still flat, but it will not give you idlis. It will give you wet rice paste.

Most founders pour the batter too early.

Sanjay and the Museum

Sanjay is a founder I have worked with for the last six years. He runs a small but distinguished museum design firm in Bangalore — the kind of company that gets hired to design exhibits for science museums, history museums, corporate visitor centers. They have done work in India, the UAE, Singapore, and most recently Kenya.

Sanjay's business is unusual because his sales cycle is measured in years, not months. A museum project takes eighteen months from the first conversation to the signed contract. Then the project itself takes two to three years. Then the museum opens, and only then does Sanjay get the visibility that leads to the next project.

For the first four years of his company, his revenue chart looked like a heartbeat monitor. He would have a great year, then a flat year, then a great year, then two flat years. Investors would not touch him. His parents asked him every Diwali whether he was going to get a real job.

I sat with Sanjay one evening on his terrace, looking out at the Bangalore skyline. He was in the middle of one of his flat years. He had two projects in delivery and no projects in negotiation, and he was, for the first time, considering whether to wind the company down.

I asked him a question I have asked many founders since. "If I told you that for the next five years your revenue would grow at exactly twelve percent a year, no spikes, no crashes, just twelve percent a year, would you still want to do this work?"

He thought about it for a long time. Then he said: "Yes. I would. I love this work."

"Then what is the problem?"

The problem, it turned out, was not the slow growth. The problem was that he had been comparing himself to founders in adjacent industries — software founders, e-commerce founders — whose growth curves were structurally different from his own. He had been measuring himself against a curve that did not apply to his business.

Sanjay's business is not a software business. It will never grow like a software business. It is a craft business with a long cycle. The right comparison is to a small architecture firm, or a high-end consulting firm, or a boutique production company. By those standards, he was doing well. By the standards of someone running a SaaS company in San Francisco, he was failing.

He was failing only because he was measuring himself wrong.

We changed the metrics. We changed the way he reported to himself, monthly, on his own performance. We changed the way he answered, at dinners, when people asked him how the business was going. He stopped saying "growing slowly" and started saying "deepening." It was a true word for what he was doing.

His revenue today is about three times what it was on that terrace. He has done more interesting work in the last three years than in the previous six combined. He sleeps fine.

The lesson is not "be patient." The lesson is "measure yourself against the right tree." A bamboo grove and a teak forest do not grow on the same calendar. Both are healthy. Both are valuable. They just live different lives.

🌱 🌱 🌱

Vikram, the Undermining COO

I want to tell a harder story now, because the season-of-no-growth chapters are also often the chapters when something is wrong inside the company that is not yet visible from the outside.

Becoming the Seed

Vikram was the chief operating officer at a company I worked with closely. The founder was a brilliant, kind, slightly conflict-avoidant woman who had built a beautiful product and a loyal customer base. She had hired Vikram in year three to help her scale operations. On paper, Vikram was perfect. He had run operations at two larger companies. He came with strong references. He was articulate, decisive, and well-dressed.

For the first year, things seemed to go well. Then growth slowed. Then several of the founder's longest-serving employees began to leave, one after another, with vague reasons. Then a few customers complained, in private channels, about a coldness that had not been there before.

I was helping the founder think through what was wrong. We sat in her office one Saturday morning, with the door closed, and I asked her a question. "When was the last time you and Vikram disagreed in front of the team?"

She thought about it. She could not remember.

"When was the last time you and Vikram disagreed in private?"

She thought about it. She could remember several times — but each one had ended with her conceding.

I asked her to walk me through the most recent five major decisions her company had made. Who had made each one. Who had been in the room. Who had pushed back.

The pattern was unmistakable. On every operational decision in the last eight months, Vikram had won. On every disagreement, the founder had ceded. Several decisions that the founder had, on reflection, disagreed with at the time — including a decision to let go of one of her oldest employees — had been framed by Vikram as "the obvious next step" and she had not pushed back.

Vikram was not malicious. He was not trying to take over the company. He was simply doing what he had been hired to do, with the authority he had been given, and the founder's natural avoidance of conflict had let his judgment quietly replace hers across the operating layer of the business.

The company had stopped being hers. It had become his.

The hard conversation took six months. The founder rebuilt her own authority slowly. She reasserted decisions in areas she cared about. She let Vikram own areas where his judgment was genuinely better. They renegotiated their working agreement. Vikram, to his credit, took the conversation well, though I think it surprised him.

A year later, the company was growing again. Two of the longtime employees who had left came back. The founder told me, on a long call: "I almost let someone else become the founder of my own company because I did not want to have one uncomfortable meeting with him."

The seasons when nothing seems to be growing are sometimes the seasons when something is being eaten from the inside. Look at the roots. Sometimes the leaves are the same color, but the roots are being chewed on by something you have not yet identified.

🍓 🍓 🍓

Thabo and the Cape Town Edtech

Thabo runs an edtech company out of Cape Town that builds curriculum-aligned learning content for South African secondary schools. He started it eight years ago. He has lived through three full no-growth seasons.

Thabo's first no-growth season was structural. He had built a product for private schools, but the private school market in South Africa was small. He had to either expand into the public school market — which had different procurement, different budgets, different politics — or stay small and profitable. He chose to expand. The first attempt failed. The second attempt, three years in, succeeded.

His second no-growth season was about distribution. He had a great product, but he could not get into enough schools fast enough. He spent a year experimenting with sales channels — direct sales, partnerships with publishers, district-level deals. The first two failed. The district-level model worked, but it took eighteen months to validate.

His third no-growth season was about people. His head of content left. His CTO got a better offer from a larger company. He had to rebuild the senior team while the company itself was growing. The new team took nine months to gel. During those nine months, the company did not innovate. It just operated.

I have known Thabo through all three seasons. The thing I admire most about him is his refusal to dramatize them.

Other founders, when they are in a no-growth season, narrate it constantly. They post on LinkedIn about resilience. They write blog essays about hard times. They talk about it at dinners until their friends are tired of the topic. The narration becomes a kind of substitute for the work.

Thabo does not narrate. He just keeps farming. When I asked him, last year, how he had survived the three flat seasons without losing his mind, he shrugged. "I am not building a story about myself. I am building a school content business. The story is for after."

The founders I have seen survive long seasons of no growth are the ones who are not constantly performing the difficulty of the season for an external audience. They put their head down. They do the next right thing. They do not announce. They just continue.

This is harder than it sounds. The instinct to be seen, especially in difficulty, is strong. Resist it.

The Hidden Math of Compounding

A quiet point about math.

Most founders, in a no-growth year, lose patience because they imagine the next year will also be a no-growth year, and the year after that. They look forward and see only flatness, and they conclude that they must do something dramatic to break out.

But businesses do not actually grow linearly. They grow in steps. A no-growth year is often the soil being prepared for a step-up year. The hire you made who will not produce results until quarter three. The product you launched that will not have customer evidence until next year. The geography you opened that will not break even for eighteen months. The brand you have been quietly building that will start delivering inbound leads in a year.

If you imagine each year independently, and you see only the current flatness, you will lose patience. If you imagine the compounding underneath, and you see what is being planted, you will be willing to wait.

I once asked Thatha, when I was much older, how he survived years where the rains were poor and the harvest was small.

He said: "A bad year is not a bad year. A bad year is when you find out what you were doing wrong in the good years, and you fix it for the next good year."

Most no-growth years are diagnostic years. The growth was hiding something. The flatness reveals it. If you use the flatness well — to fix what was hidden — the next growth season will be cleaner, healthier, more durable.

This requires you to stop running long enough to look. Most founders cannot stop running. They confuse activity with progress. In a flat year, they activity-themselves into deeper trouble.

If your year is flat, and you have looked honestly and the business is sound and the trajectory is just slow, the right response is often: do less, look more, fix what is hidden. The next compounding season will surprise you.

※ ※ ※

What Founders Get Wrong About Bad Quarters

Three patterns I have seen, repeatedly, that you may want to watch out for:

The first pattern is over-reaction to a single bad quarter. A founder has one quarter where growth slows. Instead of asking why, they restructure. They fire someone. They change the strategy. They pivot. Six months later, when the underlying issue turns out to have been a one-time customer event, they have torn up a healthy company in response to a temporary signal.

The right response to a single bad quarter is investigation, not action. Find out what happened. If it is structural, address it. If it is one-time, do nothing. Most quarters are noise. A few are signal. The discipline is in telling them apart.

The second pattern is under-reaction to a slow series of bad quarters. A founder has three quarters in a row of slowing growth, but each quarter has a plausible local explanation — a holiday season, a key hire transition, a one-time customer issue. They tell themselves a different story each quarter. They do not do the harder work of asking whether the three explanations together point to something deeper.

The right response to three bad quarters in a row is to assume there is a structural issue and to look for it actively. The local explanations are usually true and are also usually a distraction from the larger truth.

The third pattern is what I call founder weather forecasting — the founder treats every quarter as if their personal mood about the business is the truth about the business. In a good quarter, they tell investors the company is on a rocket ship. In a bad quarter, they tell them the company is in trouble. Investors and employees lose the ability to calibrate to the founder's signals because the signals are too noisy.

The right response is to develop, internally, a steadier read of the business. The numbers tell a slower truth than the founder's mood. Trust the numbers. Update your internal narrative quarterly, not weekly.

A Note on Identity in the Slow Years

The hardest part of a slow year is not the business. It is what the slow year does to your identity.

When the company is growing, you are a successful founder. When the company is flat, you are — what? A founder running a small business? A founder who used to be promising? A person who is failing in slow motion?

This is the storm that wrecks the most founders. Not the business storm. The identity storm.

I have watched founders lose their composure in flat years, not because the business was actually in trouble, but because they could not sit with the uncertainty about who they were. They needed the company to be performing for them to feel okay. When it was not performing, they were not okay.

The work, in the slow years, is to disentangle yourself from the company's quarter-by-quarter performance. The company is the company. You are you. The company will have flat years. You are still you in those years. Your worth as a person, as a parent, as a friend, as a citizen, is not on the income statement.

I learned this slowly. I learned it from Thatha, who once had a year where the rains failed and the rice harvest was less than half of normal. He did not become less of a man that year. He became more of one. He found work as a day laborer for two months to bring in cash. He repaired tools that he had been planning to replace. He visited neighbors more than usual. He carried himself the same way he always had.

When I asked him about it later, he said: "The land does not know who I am. I am who I am whether the harvest is good or bad."

Becoming the Seed

Hold on to who you are when the harvest is small. The harvest will turn. You will be there for it.

🍎 🍎 🍎

Seeds to Plant

For the slow seasons:

What are you measuring yourself against, and is the comparison fair? Are you holding a teak tree to the calendar of a bamboo grove, or vice versa? Who in your industry, with your business model, has actually grown the way you are expecting your company to grow — and over what time horizon?

In the last bad quarter or year, what did you do? Did you investigate, or did you act? If you acted, did the action address what was actually wrong, or did it address what was easiest to do?

Is there a Vikram in your company — someone whose authority is quietly displacing yours? When was the last time you disagreed with them in front of the team? When was the last time you disagreed with them in private and held your ground?

If your company grew exactly twelve percent a year for the next five years — no spikes, no crashes — would you still want to do this work? If yes, what is the problem? If no, what would you do instead?

In your slowest year, who were you outside the company? Did you like that person? If you did, you have built a foundation that the harvest cannot take from you.

Becoming the Seed

Chapter 10: Return to Simplicity

On the Things You Do Not Need

I am writing this section in a small house we built two years ago on a piece of land outside Pollachi, about four hours from Chennai. It is not a farm. It is a small plot — about an acre — with mango trees that were already there when we bought it, a vegetable patch we have been slowly establishing, and a low single-story house with a verandah where I sit in the evenings.

There is no television in this house. There is electricity, and there is a small inverter for when the power goes out. There is a single ceiling fan in each room. The kitchen has a gas stove, a refrigerator, and a small stone counter where my wife, when she is here, makes filter coffee in the mornings.

That is most of it.

The first time we stayed here for a full week, I noticed something I had not noticed for years. I was bored. Not in a bad way. In the way I used to be bored as a child in our village, when the afternoon had nothing in it and I had to invent the next thing to do. The boredom was uncomfortable for the first two days. By the third day, it had turned into something else. I started reading more slowly. I started noticing when the light shifted in the afternoon. I started having long, unhurried conversations with my wife that did not have a topic.

My phone still worked here. Email still arrived. But the rhythm of the place was different from Chennai, and the rhythm changed me before I changed it.

There is a thing that happens to founders in their tenth year, or their fifteenth, that I did not understand until it happened to me. The thing is this: you discover that most of what you spent your life acquiring was not necessary. Some of it was actively in the way.

This chapter is about the long return.

What I Spent Money On That I Should Not Have

I want to be specific, because the abstract version of this story sounds like a yoga retreat brochure.

In my mid-thirties, when my consulting business was doing well, I bought things. I bought a larger apartment in a building with a swimming pool I never used. I bought a second car that mostly sat in the basement parking. I bought watches I have not worn in five years. I bought membership in a club whose dining room I visited four times in three years.

I told myself, at the time, that these things were appropriate to my station. I had earned them. I should enjoy them.

What I now know is that they were not enjoyments. They were performances. I was performing — for relatives who had once doubted me, for old classmates who had said I would not amount to much, for some imagined younger version of myself who would be impressed by what the older version had accumulated. The performances cost real money, and real attention, and real time. None of the audiences I was performing for were watching as closely as I imagined.

The car I should not have bought sat for so long that the battery died and the engine seized. We sold it eventually for less than half what I had paid for it. The apartment I should not have bought was beautiful and lonely. We moved out of it, three years ago, into a smaller place in a quieter neighborhood, and I have not missed a single square foot.

Thatha never bought anything he did not use. He had two pairs of dhotis. He had three shirts. He had one good pair of leather sandals, and one pair of rubber sandals for the rains. He had a small steel watch that had been a gift from my father on his fortieth birthday. That was the entire wardrobe of a man who lived to be eighty-four.

He was not poor. He had money. He had savings. He owned land. He chose, deliberately, not to buy things he did not need. I asked him once why. He said: "Each thing you own owns a small part of you. If you own too many things, you have very little left of yourself."

I did not understand this for thirty years. Now I understand it.

Proportion

Becoming the Seed

A founder I know in Tokyo built a company to two thousand employees over eighteen years, sold it to a larger conglomerate, and now runs a fourteen-seat café in a quiet neighborhood. She bakes the bread herself. She is closed on Mondays and Tuesdays.

I asked her, when I visited the café last autumn, why she had chosen the smaller life.

She said: "When I was running my company, I had two thousand employees and I knew about thirty of them. Now I have no employees, and every person who walks into this café, I know."

She is not running the café for money. She is running it for proportion. The size of her old life had grown beyond her capacity to be present in it. The size of her new life fits inside her attention.

Most founders never ask whether the size of their company is in proportion to the size of their attention, their care, the life they are trying to live. They assume bigger is always better. They assume more people, more revenue, more presence, more travel, is the right direction. It is sometimes. It is not always. Past a certain size, you stop being able to hold what you are holding, and you are losing things you do not yet realize you are losing.

I am not telling you to sell your company and open a café. I am telling you to ask, honestly, whether what you are building is in proportion to what you can love. If it is, build more. If it is not, the answer is not always more building. Sometimes the answer is to stop and stand still.

🍎 🍎 🍎

The Things Founders Do Not Need

A specific list, because abstract advice slides off.

You do not need to be on every podcast that invites you. The marginal podcast is rarely worth the time. Pick the one that matches your audience and decline the rest with a polite note.

You do not need to be on every panel at every conference. Most conference panels are thinly attended and do not move your business. They move your ego. Decline the ones that do not have a clear business case. Your time is not free.

You do not need to know everyone in your industry. There is a fantasy in startup culture that the most networked founder wins. This is not true. The founder who knows the right twelve people deeply, and stays in touch with them, will outlast the founder who knows three hundred people superficially.

You do not need a personal brand on social media that takes ten hours a week to maintain. Most founders' personal brands do not generate revenue commensurate with the time spent on them. They generate validation. Validation is a calorie-poor food. It fills you up but does not nourish you.

Becoming the Seed

You do not need to attend every team event, every customer dinner, every investor gathering. Your absence, occasionally, is a useful signal. It tells your team that you trust them. It tells your investors that you have boundaries. It tells you that the world does not end when you are not there.

You do not need to read every business book that comes out, or follow every commentary thread, or memorize every framework. Pick a small number of teachers and stay with them. Depth beats breadth in your reading the same way it does everywhere else.

You do not need an office that impresses people. The team's morale will not be improved by marble. Spend the money on the team instead.

You do not need a title that announces you. "Founder" is sufficient. The founders who insist on being called "Chairman and Chief Visionary Officer" are usually compensating for something the title cannot give them.

You do not need to be busy. Busyness is not a measure of importance. It is often a measure of poor calendar discipline. The founders I respect most are often the ones with empty afternoons, because they have built systems that do not require their constant intervention.

The list is longer than this. You can write your own version of it. The exercise itself is useful.

What Came Back When I Cleared Things Out

What was on the other side of the simplification surprised me, because the simplification is not its own reward.

When we sold the larger apartment, my wife and I had two months between the sale and the move into the smaller place. We rented a small service apartment near my office. It had two rooms and almost no furniture. For two months, we lived with very little.

I noticed three things, in order.

First, I noticed how much faster the mornings were. With fewer choices about what to wear, fewer rooms to pass through, fewer surfaces to clean, the morning collapsed from ninety minutes to forty. The reclaimed time went mostly to coffee on the small balcony, where my wife and I talked about nothing in particular.

Second, I noticed how much less I was thinking about the things in the larger apartment. They had taken up mental space I had not understood was occupied. The car in the basement that I should have been driving more. The spare bedroom I had been meaning to convert into a study. The watch I had been meaning to take to be serviced. Each of these small open loops had been costing me a small piece of attention, every day, for years. When the loops closed, the attention came back.

Third, I noticed that I was sleeping better. I cannot fully account for this. I think it was because the smaller space was easier to keep tidy, and a tidy space is easier to fall asleep in. I think it was also because the smaller space had less of what my therapist would later call "performance load" — fewer reminders that I was a person who had to be impressive.

When we moved into the smaller permanent apartment, I deliberately did not refurnish to match the old place. We brought what we needed. We left what we did not. Three years later, I have not added much.

Thatha would not have used the word "minimalism." He would not have known the word. But he would have understood the principle. He kept his life small enough to look at all the parts of it. There were no parts of his life he did not know about. There were no rooms he had not entered in months. There were no relationships he had let lapse because he did not have time. He was the steward of a small kingdom, and he was a good steward because the kingdom was small enough to steward well.

I am trying to learn this, late.

༃ ༃ ༃

The Conversation I Had With My Wife About How Much Was Enough

This conversation was hard. I think most founder marriages need a version of it.

We had it about four years ago, on a long drive back from a wedding in Coimbatore. The road was empty. The conversation had been building for a while.

She asked me, in the simplest way: "Arun, how much money do we need? When are we done?"

Becoming the Seed

I started to give her the founder answer. The "we are building something larger than money" answer. The "the next round will let us do x and then we can talk about it" answer.

She let me finish. Then she said: "I am not asking what the company needs. I am asking what we need."

I did not have a number. I had never thought about it. The company had become the answer to every question, including the questions about us.

We did not solve it on the drive. We came back to it, in pieces, over the next several months. We worked, eventually, with a financial advisor who helped us put real numbers on what we needed for the rest of our lives. It was a smaller number than I had assumed. We were already past it.

The realization that we were already past it changed how I worked. I did not stop working. But I stopped working as if my survival depended on the next quarter. I started working because I wanted to, on things I cared about, with people I respected, at a pace that did not consume me. The business itself did not change much. I changed.

I think most founders never have this conversation. They keep working as if survival is at stake, long after survival is not at stake. The invented urgency consumes years of their lives. They reach an age where they look up and ask, with surprise, where the time went.

It went into solving for a problem that had been solved.

If you have never asked yourself, with real numbers, how much is enough — please ask. Ask your spouse. Ask your financial advisor. Ask yourself in a quiet hour. The number, when you find it, will be smaller than you think, and the freedom of knowing the number will be larger than you can currently imagine.

A Caution Against Performative Simplicity

A caution, because the back-to-roots conversation has its own version of performance, and it can be just as hollow as the original.

There are founders I have met who have made simplicity into a brand. They post photos of their farm. They talk in interviews about how they have left the rat race. They use the words "intentional" and "presence" a lot. They are still, beneath the new packaging, performing.

Performative simplicity is not simplicity. It is the same hunger for an audience, served with different garnish.

Real simplicity does not announce itself. The Tokyo café owner does not post about her café. Thatha did not lecture us about his two dhotis. The people who have actually returned to a smaller life are usually the people you would not know had returned, unless you spent enough time with them to notice.

The test is private. When you reduce something in your life — a possession, an obligation, a performance — do you feel relief, or do you feel a faint disappointment that no one will know? The relief is real simplification. The disappointment is the same old hunger, in a different costume.

I have caught myself in the disappointment many times. I have caught myself wanting credit for a sacrifice. The credit is not the point. The freedom is the point. Be free in private first. The public will not know, and that is the entire point.

What Returning to Roots Actually Means

The phrase "back to roots" has been used so loosely that it has lost most of its meaning. Let me try to give it back some.

Going back to your roots is not about geography. It is not about moving to a village or buying a farm or wearing traditional clothing. Those can be parts of it, but they are not it.

Going back to your roots is about returning to the version of yourself that existed before you started accumulating other people's expectations. The you that existed at twelve, or fifteen, or seventeen, before the world began telling you who you should be in order to succeed. That earlier self had instincts, preferences, things that delighted them, things that bored them, things they wanted to spend their days on.

Becoming the Seed

Most founders, by the time they are forty, have buried that earlier self under a pile of acquired identities. The successful founder identity. The serial entrepreneur identity. The thought leader identity. The angel investor identity. Each acquired identity covered the original one a little more.

Going back to your roots is digging that earlier self up. Asking it what it wants now. Listening, even when the answer is inconvenient.

For me, the answer was: I want to spend more time with my wife. I want to grow vegetables, badly, on a small piece of land. I want to read books that have nothing to do with business. I want to mentor a small number of founders, deeply, instead of a large number superficially. I want to be the kind of grandfather Thatha was, when my time comes.

None of these answers required me to leave Chennai or sell my businesses. They required me to rebalance my time and attention so that the original self could breathe again.

If you are forty, or forty-five, or fifty, and you have not had this conversation with your earlier self in a long time, please have it. Sit somewhere quiet. Ask the twelve-year-old version of you what they would like to spend a Saturday on. Listen to the answer. Then ask yourself what is preventing you from giving them that Saturday.

Whatever the answer is, it is probably less unmovable than you currently believe.

Seeds to Plant

Try this:

What is in your life right now that you do not need? Make a literal list. Possessions, obligations, performances, memberships, subscriptions, relationships you are maintaining out of habit rather than care. The list itself will be revealing.

What would you cut if you knew no one would notice the cut? The fact that no one will notice is the test, not the obstacle.

How much money do you actually need for the rest of your life? Have you ever calculated it with someone qualified to help? If you have, is the number you are working toward larger than the number you actually need? If yes, why?

Who were you at fifteen — what did that person love, want to spend time on, look forward to? Are there pieces of that person you can give Saturdays back to, without rearranging the rest of your life?

What is one thing you could remove from your life this week — one meeting, one obligation, one possession — and not miss in three months? Remove it. See what comes back.

The land does not know who you are. You are who you are whether you are wearing the costume or not.

Chapter 11: The Farmer's Solitude

On Inner Life, Family, and the Self You Are Becoming

I have written, in earlier chapters, about the loneliness of the founder's chair. About the things you cannot say to your team, your investors, or your customers. About the people who do not understand and cannot be expected to.

This chapter goes one layer deeper than that. It is about the inner life that runs alongside the company — the marriage, the family, the body, the mind, the questions about who you are becoming as a person, not as a founder.

I almost did not write this chapter. It is the chapter I have the least authority on, because I have made the most mistakes in it. Every paragraph, I had to push past the voice that said: who are you to write about this when you have failed at it. I kept writing because the founders who never have this conversation, even with themselves, are the ones who lose the most.

I do not want you to lose what I almost lost.

What I Almost Lost

Becoming the Seed

You met my wife earlier, in the chapter where I admitted to almost losing my marriage to ambition. I gave her the pseudonym Nila there. I will keep using it here.

Five years into the consulting business, six years into our marriage, I had built a life in which Nila was a supporting character. I was the protagonist. The company was the central plot. She had a small but important role: she kept the home, she kept me functioning, she occasionally asked questions that I treated as interruptions.

I did not call her a supporting character at the time. I did not even think it. But that is what she was, in the structure of my days. The hours of my life were going to the company. The leftover hours were going to her. She was getting the leftovers, and she was, for years, gracious about it.

The Sunday in the coffee shop, which I described earlier, was the day she stopped being gracious. She did not yell. She did not cry. She just told me, in a steady voice, that she was tired of being a supporting character in someone else's story, and that if I wanted her to remain in the story at all, I would need to rewrite the part.

I would like to tell you I rewrote it immediately. I did not. I rewrote it slowly, and badly, and I had to redo it several times before the rewrite held.

The first rewrite was cosmetic. I started coming home earlier. I put my phone away during dinner. I asked her about her day. These were good things. They were not the rewrite. The rewrite was deeper.

The deeper rewrite was about who I considered the most important person in the room. For years, the most important person in the room had been the customer, or the investor, or the team. Nila had been somewhere lower down the list. The deeper rewrite required me to put her, durably, at the top. Not in the cosmetic sense of saying so. In the sense of making the actual decisions of my life — what to take on, what to refuse, when to travel, when to be home, what to say yes to, what to say no to — with her at the top of the list of things being optimized for.

This took years.

I would like to tell you I have it right now. I do not have it right now. I have it more right than I had it ten years ago. I expect to have it more right ten years from now than I have it today. The work is not over.

If you are a founder reading this, and you have a partner, please do not assume that the partner is being patient because they are content. Patience and contentment are different. Many partners in founder marriages are patient for years, and then one day they are not, and the not is sudden and irreversible.

Find out, before that day, whether your partner is content. Ask them. Listen to the answer. Then change what needs to change, even if changing it costs you something at work. The cost at work, whatever it is, is smaller than the cost of losing the person who was waiting up for you.

The Identity Trap

There is a trap that founders fall into that has cost more marriages, more friendships, more health, and more sanity than any market downturn. The trap is this: the founder begins to believe that they are their company.

It happens slowly. In the first year, the company is something you are doing. By the third year, the company is something you are. By the seventh year, you and the company are indistinguishable in your own mind. When the company has a good week, you feel like a good person. When the company has a bad week, you feel like a failed one.

You will recognize the trap, if you are in it, by a few symptoms. You cannot describe yourself to a stranger without mentioning the company. You cannot enjoy a vacation because the company is not with you. You cannot listen to criticism of the company without feeling personally attacked. You cannot imagine the next ten years of your life without the company in it. You become bored, in social settings, by people who are not interested in what you are building.

I had every one of these symptoms. I have had to work, deliberately, to dismantle each one.

The dismantling started with a simple exercise that a friend taught me. He asked me to describe myself for thirty seconds without mentioning my work, my title, or my company. Just me, as a person.

I struggled. I made it about eight seconds before I ran out of things to say.

He pointed out, gently, that I had built a self that was almost entirely contained inside a company that I did not own outright, that was subject to market forces I did not control, that would one day either be sold or shut down or pass to other people. The self I had built was in a building I did not own, on land I had leased, that I would one day have to vacate.

What would be left of me when I vacated?

This was an uncomfortable question. I have been working on the answer for years. The answer is being built, slowly: the relationships I am tending to outside the company, the practices I do every day that have nothing to do with work, the books I am reading that are not business books, the small piece of land we are slowly cultivating, the friendships I am keeping warm with people who do not care what I do for a living.

I am building a self that will outlast my work. You should be doing the same thing. Start now. The longer you wait, the harder it gets.

Thatha had this naturally. He was a farmer, but he was many other things. He was a husband. A grandfather. A reader of the local newspaper at the village tea shop. A friend of two old men he had known since they were boys. A keeper of the small temple at the corner of our street. A teller of stories to neighborhood children on summer evenings. The farm was his work. It was not him. When the farm had a bad year, he was still all of those other things, and the bad year did not unmake him.

You need other rooms in the house of who you are. Build them now, while you have time, while there is still room in your week to build them. You will need them.

🍎 🍎 🍎

Ravi Kapoor and the Singapore Expat

Let me introduce a founder I will call Ravi Kapoor. He is an Indian founder who has spent the last twelve years in Singapore building a fintech business that serves the Southeast Asian remittance market. By any external measure, he is a success. The company is profitable, growing, well-funded.

I met Ravi at a small dinner three years ago. We sat next to each other and talked about everything except work for the first hour. Late in the evening, when most of the table had moved on to other conversations, he leaned over and said, very quietly: "I do not know who I am anymore."

I asked him what he meant.

He said: "I have been in Singapore for twelve years. I left India to build this business. My parents are getting old in Delhi. My oldest friends are in India. My wife and

I have built a life here that is comfortable but not fully ours. My children are growing up speaking English with a Singaporean accent. They visit India in summers and they are tourists there. We are not Indian anymore. We are not Singaporean either. We are nothing in particular. The only thing that holds us in place is the company."

We talked for another hour. The conversation has stayed with me.

Ravi's situation is increasingly common. Founders who have moved across borders to build their companies — whether to the United States, the Gulf, Singapore, the United Kingdom — often find themselves, a decade in, with a company in one country and a sense of self that does not fully belong to either the country they left or the country they are in. The company becomes the only stable identity. When the company is the only stable identity, you cannot afford for the company to ever be in trouble, because if the company is in trouble, you have nothing else to hold on to.

This is dangerous.

I worked with Ravi over the next year on a small set of practical commitments. He started spending one full week a quarter back in Delhi, with his parents, not working. He joined a small community of Indian families in Singapore who met every Sunday for cooking and conversation in Hindi. He started a practice of writing, by hand, to two old friends from his school days in Lucknow — long letters, twice a year. He took his children, for the first time, on a three-week trip through small towns in Uttar Pradesh, with no business attached.

A year later, he told me: "The company is the same. I am different. I have somewhere to put my feet down that is not a balance sheet."

If you are a founder living far from where you grew up, please pay attention to this. The company will not be enough to hold you in place forever. Build other things that hold you in place. Visit the places that made you. Stay in touch with the people who knew you before. Teach your children where they came from, even if they are growing up somewhere else. The roots cannot be portable. They have to live somewhere.

The Therapy Taboo

What follows is uncomfortable to write, because it goes against what many founders — particularly Indian and Asian and Middle Eastern founders — were taught.

If you are a founder, and you have not seen a therapist, you may want to consider seeing one.

I know. I know all the objections. I had them too. Therapy is for people with serious problems, not for people like me. I can think through my own issues. My family will think I am weak. My partner will worry. My team will lose confidence in me if they find out. The therapist will not understand my world. I do not have time. It is expensive. It is self-indulgent. There are people with real problems and I am fine.

I held these objections for years. I started therapy four years ago, after Nila gently pushed me into it following an episode I will not describe in detail except to say that I did not handle a difficult quarter well, and the way I did not handle it was visible to my family in ways I had not intended.

The therapy was strange at first. The first three sessions were spent, mostly, with me explaining to the therapist what my work was, why it mattered, why my situation was different from his other clients. He listened patiently. In the fourth session, he asked me a question that broke something open. The question was: "When was the last time you felt safe?"

I did not have an answer. I had not felt safe in a long time. I had been operating on managed fear, masked as competence, for so many years that I had forgotten what its absence felt like.

The work since then has been slow. I am not a different person. I am a more honest one. I have learned to recognize when I am not okay. I have learned to ask for help before things become a crisis. I have learned that some of the patterns I had inherited — from my father, from his father, from the broader culture I grew up in — were not laws of nature. They were patterns. Patterns can be examined. Sometimes they can be changed.

Thatha never went to therapy. He would not have known the word. What he had instead was a village — a small number of men who had known him since boyhood, who walked the same field bunds at dusk, who sat in the same tea shop at four in the afternoon, who did not need to be told when something was wrong. That is not therapy, exactly. But it did some of the same work. He was known, and held, by people whose role in his life was not transactional.

Most of us no longer have that. The old structures that held men together — long friendships rooted in place, village elders, the joint family system — have largely dissolved. The structures have not been replaced. We are walking alone in a way our grandparents would have found incomprehensible.

If you do not have the kind of village Thatha had, find a therapist. If the word "therapist" feels too clinical, find a coach, a spiritual director, a long-tenured mentor — someone whose only job is to listen to you without an agenda. You need this. The fact that you think you do not need this is often the strongest signal that you do.

🌱 🌱 🌱

What Marriages Need That No One Tells Founders

I am going to make some specific observations, from my own marriage and from the marriages I have watched closely over the years. These are not universal. Take what is useful.

Becoming the Seed

Marriages need ordinary time, not just special time. The anniversary dinner is nice. The vacation is nice. They are not what the marriage runs on. The marriage runs on the unstructured Wednesday evening when nothing in particular happens and you are present for each other. If your weeks have no Wednesdays, your marriage is in trouble even if your anniversaries are good.

Marriages need each partner to be interested in the other partner's interior life. Not the events of the day. The interior life. What they are afraid of. What they are hopeful about. What is bothering them that they have not told anyone. Most founder spouses know an enormous amount about the founder's company and almost nothing about the founder's interior. Most founders know very little about their spouse's interior. The interior conversation is the one that holds the marriage together.

Marriages need a shared project that is not the company. The children, if there are children. The home you are slowly building. The travel you are doing together. The book you are reading aloud at night. The garden you are planting. There has to be something the two of you are building together, on which the company has no claim. Without it, the marriage becomes an arrangement that supports the company. With it, the marriage becomes a thing of its own.

Marriages need each partner to be willing to be wrong, in front of the other, and to apologize without cleverness. Founders are bad at this. We are trained, in our work, to defend our positions, to explain why we are right, to manage perceptions. These skills are toxic in a marriage. If your partner says you have hurt them, the right response is not to explain why their reading is incorrect. The right response is "I am sorry, tell me more." If you cannot do this, your partner will eventually stop telling you things. When they stop telling you things, the marriage is hollowing out, even if it looks intact from the outside.

Marriages need the founder to occasionally do nothing, in the partner's company, without performing relaxation. Sit on the couch. Read a book. Be present without being entertaining. The performance of being present is exhausting for both of you. The actual presence is restful.

I have failed at most of these things, repeatedly, and continue to fail at some of them. The point is not that I have figured this out. The point is that I now know what to aim at. Most founders never even articulate the aim. They mean to be a good partner, but they have not thought concretely about what that requires. The thinking is the first step.

The Body You Are Living In

A short section, but a load-bearing one.

You will not run your company forever. Some of the founders I have watched were not able to enjoy what they built because their bodies gave out before the company did — heart attacks at fifty-two, diabetes managed badly through years of stress eating, chronic back pain, insomnia that compounded into cognitive decline, alcohol that started as a reward and became a problem. These are not personal failings. They are predictable consequences of the founder lifestyle. If you do not actively work against them, they will happen to you with statistical regularity.

The work is not complicated. Sleep. Move every day. Eat food that did not come out of a wrapper. Drink less. See a doctor every year. Find a way to manage stress that does not depend on numbing it.

I am repeating these for myself; I am bad at some of them. Thatha walked five kilometers a day, every day, until he was eighty-one. He ate what came out of his garden. He slept from nine to four. He lived to eighty-four with most of his teeth, all of his memory, and the use of his legs. The cumulative effect of small daily choices is the body you will live in when your work is finally done. Build one you will want to live in.

Seeds to Plant

For the inner life:

If you had to describe yourself for thirty seconds, without mentioning your work, your title, or your company, could you do it? Try it now, out loud or on paper. Notice what you find.

Becoming the Seed

When was the last time you and your partner had an unstructured Wednesday evening together, with no agenda? If it has been more than a few weeks, schedule one before you finish this chapter.

Do you have someone outside your family and your work whose only role in your life is to listen to you, without an agenda? If not, can you build that relationship? If you cannot find a person, can you find a therapist or coach who can play that role?

What are the rooms in the house of who you are, outside the company? Make a list. If the list is short, the company is bearing too much weight. Build more rooms.

If your body could write you a letter today, what would it say? Are you giving it what it needs, or are you spending it down?

The roots cannot be portable. Plant them somewhere. Stay long enough for them to grow.

Chapter 12: Growing Others

On the Quiet Work of Being Useful to Other Founders

🍒 🍒 🍒

There comes a point in a founder's life when the most interesting question is no longer how do I grow my company. It becomes how do I help the people coming up behind me grow theirs.

It is a quieter question. It does not get the headlines. It does not pay as well. It does not come with conferences and panels and prizes. It is mostly invisible work, done in cafés and on long phone calls and in the margins of other people's calendars. But it is the most important work most senior founders eventually do.

This chapter is about that work — what it looks like, how to do it without harming the people you are trying to help, what to do when they do not listen, and what I have learned about the difference between being a mentor and being a meddler.

I should warn you, before we begin, that this is the chapter in which I will tell you most plainly about my failures as a mentor, because I have made many. The failures have taught me more than the successes. I want you to have access to them.

🍒 🍒 🍒

What Mentoring Is Not

Let me first say what mentoring is not, because the word has been broadened until it has lost most of its useful meaning.

Mentoring is not lecturing. It is not telling someone, who has not asked you, what they should do. It is not posting your opinions on social media in the hope that some founder will absorb them. It is not taking the stage at a conference and reciting your views to a passive audience. These are forms of broadcasting. They have their place. They are not mentoring.

Mentoring is not transactional. It is not "I will help you in exchange for equity." That is advisorship, and it is a different relationship. Some advisorship is healthy. Some is not. But it is not mentoring. Mentoring does not have a contract.

Mentoring is not networking. It is not introducing your founder to the right people in the hope that those people will introduce you back. It is not maintaining a list of mentees you can call on later for favors. The moment your mentoring becomes a deposit you intend to withdraw, it stops being mentoring.

Mentoring is not friendship, though it can grow into friendship. The asymmetry, at least at first, is real. The mentor has experiences the mentee does not. The mentor has time and attention to give that the mentee may not be able to reciprocate for years, if ever. Pretending the relationship is symmetric does not honor it; it confuses it.

Mentoring is, at its best, a quiet, patient, deeply attentive practice of being useful to another person's growth without taking credit for it. It is a kind of farming. You plant seeds in someone else's soil. You water them when you can. You do not stand over the seeds demanding that they grow. You go away. You come back. You water again. The harvest, if there is one, belongs to the other person.

The Robotics Failure I Have Not Fully Told You About

I touched on this in an earlier chapter. It deserves more honesty here.

About eight years ago, I tried to start a robotics company with a younger co-founder I will call Suresh. I did not write about this earlier in much detail, because the failure was complicated and I did not want to use the story to make myself look better than I had been. But this is the chapter on growing others, and the story belongs in this chapter.

Suresh was, on paper, the perfect partner. He had a doctorate in robotics from a top institution. He had worked at one of the most respected hardware labs in the world. He had a clear vision for an industrial robotics product targeted at small manufacturers in India and Southeast Asia. He was technically brilliant and personally warm. I liked him.

Becoming the Seed

I joined as a co-founder, primarily to handle the business side. We raised a small seed round. We hired six engineers. We built a prototype. We had three pilot customers within a year.

The company failed eighteen months in. The failure was not technical. The product worked. The failure was relational, and the failure was largely my fault.

I had treated Suresh, from the beginning, as my mentee rather than my partner. I was older. I had more business experience. I was the one who had raised previous companies. I assumed, without ever saying it, that my judgment on business matters should overrule his. When we disagreed on pricing, on go-to-market, on hiring, I would explain why I was right. I would do this politely. I would do this in a way I thought was respectful. But the structural pattern was clear: my views won, his views did not.

Suresh did not push back, at first. He was younger. He had less business experience. He thought he was learning from me. After about a year, he stopped offering opinions in business meetings. He nodded. He executed. He retreated into the technical work.

I took this as a sign that things were going well. We were aligned, I thought. He was focusing on his strengths. We were a healthy team.

We were not a healthy team. He was disengaging, and I was confusing his disengagement with agreement.

The end came suddenly. He came to me one Friday evening and told me he was leaving. He was not angry.

He was not accusing. He was just done. He said: "Arun, I have built this company for a year and a half, and I have not made a single business decision. This is not my company. This is your company that I am building. I do not want to do that anymore."

I tried to argue. He let me argue, then said, gently: "I know you do not see it. That is part of the problem."

He left. The company collapsed within four months. I did not have the technical depth to keep building the product without him. The investors took the loss. The engineers found other jobs. I went home and did not work for two months.

The lesson I took from this — slowly, painfully, over years — is that the mentor who does not know they are mentoring is the most dangerous kind of mentor. I had been mentoring Suresh by force, without consent, in a context where he did not need a mentor. He needed a partner. By treating him as a mentee, I had taken away the very agency that would have made him a great partner.

I have watched many older founders make this mistake with younger co-founders. I have watched founders mentor people they should have been collaborating with as equals. The damage is enormous. The damage is also invisible from the inside.

If you are an older founder partnering with a younger one, please ask yourself, regularly: am I a co-founder, or am I a hidden mentor? If you are the latter, the partnership will not survive, and the survival will be your fault.

※ ※ ※

Senthil and the Café Revisited

A small mentor story that went well, because I have given you so many that did not.

Senthil is a young founder I have known for about four years. He is from a small town near Madurai. He came to Chennai for college, never went back, and started a software business about three years after graduation. The business does workforce management software for small manufacturing units. It is not glamorous. It is useful.

I met Senthil because a mutual friend asked me to spend an hour with him. The hour stretched into the first of many conversations, mostly over coffee, mostly without any particular agenda.

The thing I have most enjoyed about my mentoring relationship with Senthil is that he is a quiet listener and a slow decider. He does not respond immediately to anything I say. He goes away. He thinks about it for days, sometimes weeks. Then he comes back and tells me what he has decided. Sometimes he has decided to do what I suggested. Often he has decided to do something different. Almost always, his decision is better than what I would have done in his place.

About a year ago, we were sitting in the same café where I had once worked through the unit economics with the cardamom-tea owner. Senthil was telling me about a difficult hire he was considering — a senior salesperson from a much larger company, with a track record but with a personality that made Senthil uneasy.

I gave him my view. I told him about the times I had hired senior people whose track records were compelling and whose personalities were uneasy, and how those hires had usually gone badly. I gave him a framework I have used for years. I felt useful.

He listened carefully. He did not respond. We finished our coffee and he went home.

A week later, he called me. "Arun, I am going to hire him."

I started to push back. He stopped me, gently. "Let me tell you why."

He had thought about my framework. He had also thought about his own company, his own stage, his own gaps. He had concluded that the salesperson, despite the personality issues, would solve a specific problem that no one else available to him could solve, and that the personality issues were manageable in the specific structure he was planning to put around the role. He had a plan. He had thought about the failure modes. He had decided to take the risk with eyes open.

He hired the salesperson. The hire worked out, mostly. There were some friction points, but Senthil had anticipated them. The salesperson stayed for two years and built the sales engine the company needed.

I learned something from that conversation that I have tried to remember. The mentor's job is not to make the right decision for the mentee. The mentor's job is to give the mentee everything they need to make their own decision, and then to honor whatever decision they make.

I have failed at the second part many times. I have given founders my view, then become disappointed when they did not follow it, then withdrawn warmth in subtle ways that they could feel. This is not mentoring. This is control with extra steps.

The good mentor gives the view and then gets out of the way. The mentee will sometimes do what you suggested. They will often do something else. Both are fine. The relationship has to survive disagreement, or the relationship is not a real one.

Madhav, the Walk-Away

There is a kind of mentee who, eventually, walks away from you. Not because they are angry. Not because anything has gone wrong. Just because they have outgrown the relationship.

This is a difficult thing to experience, especially the first time. Madhav's walk-away was one of the most useful things any mentee has ever done for me.

Becoming the Seed

I met Madhav about ten years ago. He was twenty-six. He was building a small consumer-facing app that no one believed in. I believed in him, more than the app, and I told him so. We met every two or three months for the first year. The app failed. He started something else. The something else also failed. He started a third thing that worked, modestly. By the time he was thirty-one, he was running a quietly profitable business with about thirty employees.

We had been meeting regularly for five years at that point. The meetings had become ritual. We would have dinner once a quarter, talk about whatever was on his mind, and I would offer perspective. I enjoyed the meetings. I think he did too.

One evening, after dinner, he said: "Arun, I am going to take a break from our meetings for a while."

I asked why.

He said: "I have been listening to you for five years. I have learned a great deal. But I have started to notice that, in difficult moments, I think about what you would say before I think about what I think. I want to find out what I think when there is no one in my head telling me. I do not want to stop knowing you. I just want to take a break from the conversations."

I was, for a moment, hurt. I felt the small ego sting. Then I looked at him across the table and saw, clearly, that he was right. He had outgrown me, in a healthy way. The mentor relationship had given him what it could give. To stay in it longer would have been to slow his growth, not accelerate it.

I told him I understood. I told him I would be there if he ever wanted to come back. We embraced. He did not come back for four years.

When he came back, it was as a friend, not as a mentee. He had built a much larger version of his business. He had developed his own voice that did not sound like mine. He came to dinner and told me what he was thinking about, not because he wanted my opinion, but because he wanted to share his life. The relationship was deeper for the break.

If you mentor people, you have to be ready for them to walk away. The mentees who never walk away are often the ones who have not fully matured. The healthy ones leave, eventually. They come back as friends, or as peers, or sometimes not at all. All of these endings are good endings. The mentor's job includes accepting that the relationship is not a permanent fixture. It is a season. The season ends.

The Mentee Who Did Not Listen

There is also the mentee who does not listen. I have had more of these than I have had of the Senthils and the Madhavs. The mentee who does not listen is often making the right decision for themselves, even if it is the wrong decision in the abstract.

Becoming the Seed

A founder I worked with a few years ago was building a B2B SaaS product in a category becoming brutally crowded. Every venture firm was funding companies in the space. The big incumbents were launching competing products. I told him, over about a year, that he should consider repositioning — not abandoning the company, repositioning. There were adjacent categories, underserved customer segments, geographies where his product had unique advantages. I gave him three or four specific suggestions. He listened politely. He did not act on any of them.

He kept building in the original category. He kept losing deals to better-funded competitors. The company shut down about two years after our first conversation. He went on to something else, which is doing well.

I was, for a long time, frustrated. I had told him exactly what to do. He had not done it. The company had failed. I felt, in some small ungenerous part of myself, vindicated. The vindication was the wrong response. Two things were true. First, I had given him advice from outside his lived experience — I was not in his customer conversations, his investor conversations, his team meetings. His view was richer than mine. Second, the shutdown was not the worst possible outcome. He learned things in those two years that he carried into his next venture. He failed in a way that many founders need to fail before they find the thing that works.

I do not regret giving him the advice. I regret the ungenerous feeling I had when he did not take it. The mentor who needs to be right is not a mentor — they are using the mentor relationship to feel important. Notice if you are doing this. I have done it more than I would like to admit.

What the Best Mentors Have Done for Me

Before this chapter ends, an acknowledgment: I am only able to write about mentoring at all because of the people who mentored me.

The first was Thatha, who was not technically a mentor in the modern sense — he never used the word, never sat me down for a "mentoring conversation," never asked what my goals were. He was just always there, available, willing to talk, willing not to talk, willing to let me sit in his presence while he worked. The mentoring happened by osmosis, over years, and I did not realize how much of it I had absorbed until I started doing things in business and recognized his voice in my own.

The second was an older businessman in Chennai who I will not name but who, in my late twenties, took an interest in me for no reason I can name. He gave me his Saturday mornings for almost three years. He never asked for anything in return. When I tried, once, to thank him formally with a gift, he refused it. He said: "Pass it on when your turn comes."

I have been trying to pass it on ever since. I have done it imperfectly. I have made every mistake I have warned you against in this chapter. I am still learning.

The third was a senior partner at a consulting firm I worked with as a client years ago, who became, over time, a kind of professional uncle. He taught me, mostly through observation, what it looked like to be senior and useful at the same time. He never used his seniority to make me smaller. He often used it to make me larger.

Each of these people had a specific style. Thatha was silent and patient. The Saturday morning man was rigorous and direct. The consulting partner was warm and questioning. None of them tried to be anyone other than themselves. They were each fully themselves, and that was the gift they gave.

If you are starting to mentor others, do not try to copy a style. Be the version of yourself that is most useful to the person in front of you. Sometimes that is silence. Sometimes that is a hard question. Sometimes that is a long story. Sometimes that is making coffee and asking nothing.

The mentoring is not the technique. The mentoring is the presence.

Seeds to Plant

If you are starting to mentor:

Who has mentored you? Have you ever told them, plainly, what their mentoring meant? If the person is still alive, write the message this week. They may not know.

Becoming the Seed

Who are you currently mentoring, or starting to mentor? Be honest about it — including the people you mentor without realizing you are mentoring them. Are you giving them what they actually need, or what you wish someone had given you?

Are you treating any of your current co-founders or close colleagues as hidden mentees? Is your judgment quietly displacing theirs in ways they have not consented to?

When a mentee does not take your advice, what do you feel? Notice the feeling without judgment. If the feeling is frustration or vindication or smallness, sit with it. The feeling is information about you, not about them.

When did a mentor of yours do their best work for you — in a meeting, in a conversation, in a silence? What did they do? Could you do that for someone else this week?

The harvest belongs to the farmer who plants. The mentor only loaned the seeds.

Epilogue: Seeds for Tomorrow

There is one image of Thatha I have not put in this book yet. It is the one I keep for myself, mostly, because it is the one that has shaped me the most.

It is a Sunday morning. I am perhaps eleven years old. We are in the back field, the one that runs down to the small stream. He is bent over a row of seedlings — tomato, I think, though the memory has softened. He is doing something I cannot follow, with his hands, low to the ground.

I am bored, the way an eleven-year-old is bored on a Sunday morning when the adults are working and there is nothing in particular for him to do. I have been standing next to him for what feels like a long time. I want him to talk. I want him to teach me something. I want the morning to mean something so that I can take the meaning away and use it later.

He keeps working. He does not look up. After a while he says, without turning, "Sit down."

I sit down in the dirt next to him. I watch him work. He still does not say anything.

After perhaps twenty more minutes, he straightens up. He puts a hand on my shoulder. He says, "You will remember this morning when you are old."

That is all. We walk back to the house. We have lunch. The day continues.

Becoming the Seed

I did not understand, at eleven, what he meant. I am beginning to understand it now. He was not teaching me about tomatoes. He was teaching me how to be present in a morning that contained nothing dramatic. He was teaching me that some of the most important parts of a life are the parts that, in the moment, feel like nothing.

Most of your founder life will be like that morning. Long stretches in which nothing in particular is happening, and you are working, and someone next to you is also working, and there is no headline coming, and the day is just the day.

If you can learn to be present in those mornings, you will be a different kind of founder than most. You will not need the headline to feel that the work is real. You will not need the round, the exit, the press cycle, the Twitter post, to know that you are building something. You will sit in the dirt next to your work, and you will know that this is the work.

That is what I want to leave you with. Not five permissions. Not a manifesto. Just one Sunday morning, and a hand on a shoulder, and a sentence I am still unpacking forty years later.

You will remember this morning when you are old.

Sit down. Watch the work. Try to be present for it. The harvest, when it comes, is for the farmer who was actually there.

Pollachi April, 2026

About the Author

Arun Rajiah was born in Tamil Nadu. He spent his childhood between city and village, and learned most of what he now teaches from his grandfather, Seeni. He has spent more than two decades building businesses — some that worked, some that did not — and rather longer mentoring founders, mostly in private, mostly without payment.

He lives between Chennai and a small piece of land outside Pollachi, with his wife. He is, before anything else, the grandson of a farmer who never read a book on management and would have laughed at the idea of being quoted in one.

He answers letters when he can.

Acknowledgments (Continued)

To the founders whose stories appear in these pages, named and unnamed: thank you for trusting me with the seasons of your work that you did not show to others.

To my wife, called Nila in this book: there are no words. Thank you for the Sunday in the coffee shop, and for everything that came after it.

To my father, Rajiah, who was patient with a son who took the long way around, and to my aunt Mariammal, who watched me grow from the sidelines with quiet kindness.

To my grandmother, Seeniammal, who held the family together through two marriages and one long silence, and whose cooking I still measure every other meal against.

To Paramasivam, the grandfather I never met — the absence that shaped the family I was born into, and the life Thatha stepped into without ever asking to be thanked for it.

And to Thatha Seeni. Always to Thatha. The seed was yours. I have only carried it.

🌱 🌱 🌱

THE END

🌱 🌱 🌱

www.ingramcontent.com/pod-product-compliance
Lightning Source LLC
Chambersburg PA
CBHW052158220526
45471CB00004B/1726